CHARACTER ENCYCLOPEDIA
NEW EDITION

WRITTEN BY
ELIZABETH DOWSETT

CONTENTS

CHAPTER ONE

HARRY POTTER AND THE SORCERER'S STONE™

WHEN HARRY POTTER arrives at Hogwarts, he finds himself in a completely new and unknown magical world. He soon finds his place: as a student in Gryffindor house, a Seeker on the Quidditch team, and with his new friends Hermione and Ron, who always have his back.

Oliver Wood

Professor Snape

Lucian Bole

HARRY POTTER
THE BOY WHO LIVED

EVERY WITCH AND WIZARD knows the name of Harry Potter, but Harry himself has no idea there is even such a thing as magic. He is famous because, as a baby, he was the only person to survive a Killing Curse from the Dark wizard He Who Must Not Be Named.

Lightning-shaped scar was caused by the Killing Curse

UNEXPECTED BONUS
A second version of this Harry minifigure was a surprise inclusion in 2020's Diagon Alley (75978). Unlike the original, his face print has smashed glasses and cheeks dirty with Floo powder.

4 PRIVET DRIVE
Orphaned Harry lives in his cruel aunt and uncle's house, where he sleeps in a cupboard under the stairs. He always comes second to his bullying cousin, Dudley.

Plaid shirts are clothes of Muggles—non-magical folk

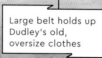

Large belt holds up Dudley's old, oversize clothes

MAGICAL FILE

YEAR: 2021
SET: 76390: Harry Potter Advent Calendar (2021)
ACCESSORIES: Wand

RUBEUS HAGRID

KEEPER OF KEYS AND GROUNDS AT HOGWARTS

MAGICAL FILE

YEAR: 2018

SETS: 75954: Hogwarts Great Hall; 75947: Hagrid's Hut: Buckbeak's Rescue; 75978: Diagon Alley

ACCESSORIES: Pink umbrella (hidden wand), lantern

HULKING HAGRID is a half-giant, but he is a big softie at heart. When Harry turns 11, Hagrid turns up with an invitation to Hogwarts School and opens Harry's eyes to a world of magic that his aunt and uncle have hidden from him.

Large pockets full of useful scraps for a groundskeeper

Regular minifigure legs fit into larger body piece

HEDWIG

Students at Hogwarts can take an animal companion. Hagrid gifts Harry a snowy owl called Hedwig. She is not only a companion, but also carries messages by Owl Post.

HAGRID'S HUT

As gamekeeper, Hagrid lives in Hogwarts' grounds. His small cozy hut, full of a jumble of tools and animals, is warm and welcoming, with a light-up LEGO® brick in the hearth.

MR. OLLIVANDER
MASTER WANDMAKER

DID YOU KNOW that it's the wand that chooses the wizard? But wands are helped on their way by Garrick Ollivander—wandmaker extraordinaire. He has been uniting wizards and witches with their wands in his busy shop on Diagon Alley for decades.

Swept-back hair piece is shared with Nearly Headless Nick

MAGICAL FILE

YEAR: 2020
SETS: 75978: Diagon Alley
ACCESSORIES: Wand

Dapper Ollivander is always neatly turned out with a cravat, waistcoat, and velvet jacket

WAND EMPORIUM
Ollivanders wand shop is a treasure trove, brimming with boxes of different wands. Each wand has a core of dragon heartstring, unicorn hair, or phoenix feather, and each one is unique.

These trousers are worn by both Ollivander minifigure variants, but each has a unique torso

WALKING TALL
In 2018, the first Ollivander minifigure towers over the microscale model of the wizarding shopping street in the Diagon Alley (40289) set.

TROLLEY WITCH

SELLER OF TASTY TREATS

Gray hair—the Trolley Witch has been working on the train for as long as anyone can remember

MAGICAL FILE

YEAR: 2018
SETS: 75955: Hogwarts Express
ACCESSORIES: Trolley

Hands clip to her trolley, nicknamed the "Honeydukes Express"

ALL ABOARD the Hogwarts Express! Every September 1 at 11 a.m., the scarlet train leaves London's King's Cross station with all the students going to Hogwarts. Also on board is the Trolley Witch who walks the aisles of the carriages, pushing her trolley of goodies to sell.

Gray leg piece is changed to matching maroon for the 2022 minifigure variant

SHOPPING TROLLEY

The Trolley Witch's cart is piled high with Cauldron Cakes, Chocolate Frogs, Jelly Slugs, Licorice Wands, Pumpkin Pasties, and Bertie Bott's Every Flavor Beans.

FANTASTICAL FARE

Harry discovers that magical sweets can be harder to eat than Muggle snacks. If you're not careful, your Chocolate Frog could leap out the window!

13

FOUNDERS OF HOGWARTS
THE MOST BRILLIANT WITCHES AND WIZARDS OF THEIR TIME

Sword of Gryffindor is goblin-made with silver and rubies

Hair piece is shared with Mr. Ollivander, but this is the only fiery colored one

MORE THAN A THOUSAND years ago, four great witches and wizards came together to establish a school. The Sorting Hat uses their combined intelligence to allocate students to the four houses that take their names and embody their values.

GODRIC GRYFFINDOR
Above all, Godric Gryffindor prized courage, bravery, and determination. These were the principles on which he founded his house, represented by a lion. Roar for Gryffindor!

Red and gold of Godric's robes live on in Gryffindor's house colors

Slytherin's locket is passed down through his descendants

Long snakelike beard

SALAZAR SLYTHERIN
Slytherin wanted Hogwarts to teach only pure-blood witches and wizards so he fell out with the other founders. Before he left, he built a secret chamber, which, legend says, holds a terrible monster.

Printed robe pattern looks like snakeskin

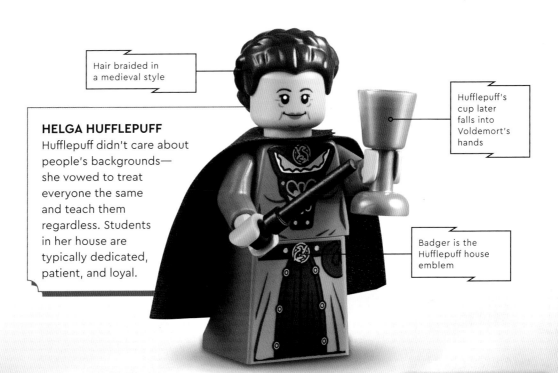

Hair braided in a medieval style

HELGA HUFFLEPUFF

Hufflepuff didn't care about people's backgrounds— she vowed to treat everyone the same and teach them regardless. Students in her house are typically dedicated, patient, and loyal.

Hufflepuff's cup later falls into Voldemort's hands

Badger is the Hufflepuff house emblem

Headpiece later becomes the legendary lost diadem of Ravenclaw

Medieval-style witch's robes

Dark blue robes with silver echo the starry ceiling of Ravenclaw's common room

MAGICAL FILE

YEAR: 2018

SET: 71043: Hogwarts Castle

ACCESSORIES: Wands, tiles with House prints, Hufflepuff's cup, Gryffindor's sword

ROWENA RAVENCLAW

Believing that "wit beyond measure is our greatest treasure," Ravenclaw based her house on wit, learning, and wisdom, and it still seeks the brightest and the most studious students.

MINERVA MCGONAGALL
HEAD OF GRYFFINDOR HOUSE

New all-in-one hat-and-hair piece

Stern expression hides caring nature

SMARTY PANTS
McGonagall's two earlier minifigures wore emerald robes with trousers and a classic witch's hat. The only difference between them is their single-sided or double-sided head.

GAME CHANGER
McGonagall teaches Transfiguration, the subject about magically changing one thing into something else. She runs a well-disciplined and happy classroom.

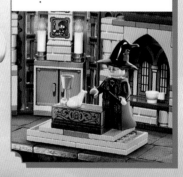

Brooch with four yellow jewels

Sloped skirt piece is new for McGonagall in 2021

STERN PROFESSOR MCGONAGALL does not stand for any nonsense, but she cares deeply for her students and treats them fairly. She is such an accomplished witch that she has become an Animagus and can turn herself into a cat.

MAGICAL FILE

YEAR: 2021

SETS: 76382: Hogwarts Moment: Transfiguration Class; 76399: Hogwarts Magical Trunk

ACCESSORIES: Wand, goblet, frog

HARRY POTTER

HOGWARTS FIRST-YEAR

Alternate face has an expression of horror

Harry wears glasses, like his father did

ARRIVING AT HOGWARTS, Harry Potter finds the home he has always wanted, and in Gryffindor he finds the family he's always dreamed of. There are not just new subjects to learn, but also the strange ways of this new wizarding world.

MAGICAL FILE

YEAR: 2021

SET: 76385: Hogwarts Moment: Charms Class

ACCESSORIES: Wand, feather

THREE'S COMPANY
During his time at Hogwarts, Harry meets his two best friends—Ron and Hermione—along with their pets, Scabbers the rat and Crookshanks the cat.

Gryffindor colors, though the Sorting Hat does consider Slytherin for Harry

SHORT LIST
The variants of Harry in Gryffindor uniform with short legs are from his first and second years. One has a scarf and blue gloves for when he takes Hedwig outside in winter.

HERMIONE GRANGER
EAGER STUDENT

MUGGLE-BORN HERMIONE is very excited about starting at Hogwarts. She's read all about it in *Hogwarts: A History*. Her parents know nothing about magic, but Hermione's clever brain is soaking up every detail about the wizarding world.

MAGICAL FILE

YEAR: 2021
SET: 76382: Hogwarts Moment: Transfiguration Class
ACCESSORIES: Wand

Fuller hair piece with bangs is used for the younger Hermione minifigures

BRIGHT SPARK
Hermione excels at her lessons, from potion-making to levitating feathers and transfiguring mice into goblets. She's always the first to put her hand up in class.

Hermione is sorted into Gryffindor, but she would have also made a good Ravenclaw

Short, unarticulated leg pieces are used for first and second years

TRUE COLORS
When first-years arrive they don't yet belong to a house so they wear plain gray and a black tie with a school badge. After sorting, they wear their house colors and tie.

RON WEASLEY
NEW HOGWARTS STUDENT

A CLASS ACT
Studying at Hogwarts brings all sorts of challenges for Ron. There are new subjects and new skills to master—like turning a rat into a goblet in a Transfiguration class.

Ginger hair runs in the Weasley family

Gray torso piece with Gryffindor badge was new for 2021

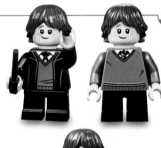

MAGICAL FILE

YEAR: 2021
SET: 76382: Hogwarts Moment: Transfiguration Class
ACCESSORIES: Wand, goblet, mouse

IN UNIFORM
Three first- and second-year Ron minifigures have short legs and variations on the Gryffindor robes. One wears general Hogwarts robes from before the Sorting Ceremony.

THE SIXTH OF SEVEN Weasley children, Ron is the youngest son and isn't used to getting much attention. At Hogwarts he makes new friends—including the famous Harry Potter, and begins to make a name for himself.

19

HERMIONE GRANGER

TOP OF THE CLASS

THANKS TO HERMIONE'S POWERS of observation, clever thinking, and memory, she, Harry, and Ron realize during their first year that Hogwarts is in great danger. One question to solve the mystery is: Who was Nicolas Flamel?

All Hermione minifigures with short legs have the same young hair style

Reversible head looks terrified at seeing Fluffy the three-headed dog

Torso has a printed pointed hood on the back

THIRST FOR KNOWLEDGE

The Library is Hermione's first port of call when she's trying to find out about Nicolas Flamel. She remembers reading that he created a magical object—the Sorcerer's Stone.

MAGICAL FILE

YEAR: 2021

SETS: 76387: Hogwarts: Fluffy Encounter; 76402: Hogwarts: Dumbledore's Office

ACCESSORIES: Wand, candle

BESPOKE CLOAKS

Hermione has an unclasped cloak for comfort in her study set and a scarf over her cloak in a chilly advent calendar set.

ALBUS DUMBLEDORE
HEADMASTER OF HOGWARTS

Earlier Dumbledore minifigures have gray hair; later ones have white

CELEBRATED WIZARD, Albus Percival Wulfric Brian Dumbledore is Headmaster of Hogwarts. He is popular and widely respected, except for among a small group who object to his inclusive policies and would like to see only pure-bloods at Hogwarts.

MAGICAL FILE

YEAR: 2018

SETS: 75954: Hogwarts Great Hall; 75964: Harry Potter Advent Calendar (2019)

ACCESSORIES: Wand, goblet

GUARDIAN ANGEL
Dumbledore watched over Harry since he was a baby, waiting for him to come to Hogwarts. He toasts Harry when he's selected for Gryffindor—Dumbledore's own house.

Dark scarlet robes were worn often during Harry's first and second years

DUMBLEDORE'S PHOENIX
The first LEGO Fawkes was brick-built rather than molded. He can be taken apart and rebuilt—just like Fawkes is reborn from the ashes after he bursts into flames.

21

NEARLY HEADLESS NICK

BADLY BEHEADED GHOST

WE PRESENT THE GHOST of Sir Nicholas de Mimsy-Porpington, but everyone just calls him Nearly Headless Nick. The knight wishes he had been properly beheaded five hundred years ago, then he could have joined the ghosts in the Headless Hunt society.

Unlike Nick's ghost, his minifigure has a fully removable head

GLOWING REPUTATION
In 2021, Nearly Headless Nick's minifigure shines in Hogwarts Chamber of Secrets (76389) with a full glow-in-the-dark body.

Embroidered doublet with ghostly silver printing

Tights and breeches were the height of fashion in the fifteenth century

GRYFFINDOR GHOST
Nearly Headless Nick is one of two house ghosts to have a minifigure. He floats around the castle, cheering on Gryffindor.

MAGICAL FILE

YEAR: 2018

SET: 75954: Hogwarts Great Hall

ACCESSORIES: His head

SEVERUS SNAPE

POTIONS PROFESSOR

Long, greasy hair

Eyebrow raised in a sneer

Sallow complexion

Purple waistcoat is as bright as Snape's clothes get

SEVERUS SNAPE is Head of Slytherin and a very skilled wizard, but he has a dubious past dabbling in the Dark Arts. He makes Harry's life a misery. When they were students at Hogwarts, Severus loved Harry's mother, but not so much Harry's dad who bullied Snape.

MAGICAL FILE

YEAR: 2021

SETS: 76383: Hogwarts Moment: Potions Class; 76402: Hogwarts: Dumbledore's Office

ACCESSORIES: Wand

DUNGEON DWELLER
Professor Snape teaches Potions in his dungeon classroom. But the job he really wants is the teaching position for Defense Against the Dark Arts.

SEVERE SNAPE
Snape's 2018 minifigure had a long printed jacket, an uncollared shirt, and his usual snarling expression.

23

MADAM HOOCH

FLYING INSTRUCTOR

Chain for Quidditch whistle

Alternate face print wears large, orange-tinted flying goggles

Tie pin of Hogwarts school crest shows no allegiance to any particular house

CRASH COURSE

Not all students are naturals at flying. In Neville Longbottom's first lesson, he falls off his broom when it goes haywire and Madam Hooch has to take him to the hospital wing.

A FLYING START

Madam Hooch's first minifigure, from 2018, wore dapper black robes and had swept-back hair rather than spikey.

Orange flying gloves

AN EXPERT on broom lore, Madam Rolanda Hooch teaches Hogwarts students to fly broomsticks. She also referees the matches for the Inter-House Quidditch Cup, always looking for a fair, clean game.

MAGICAL FILE

YEAR: 2021

SET: 76395: Hogwarts: First Flying Lesson

ACCESSORIES: Broom, wand, lantern

DRACO MALFOY
SLYTHERIN STUDENT

Double-sided head also has a snarling expression

Eyebrow raised in Draco's trademark sneer

MAGICAL FILE

YEAR: 2021

SET: 76383: Hogwarts Moment: Potions Class

ACCESSORIES: Wand, vial of potion

DRACO STARTS HOGWARTS

in the same year as Harry. He is the only child of a Black and a Malfoy—two ancient wizarding families. As pure-bloods, Draco and his parents think they are better than other wizards and witches. This leads to clashes between Draco and Harry.

Sweater has thicker stripe and deeper V-neck than previous Slytherin torsos

TRIPLE THREAT
Three other young, short-legged Draco minifigures wear the Slytherin uniform with variations on the torso printing.

CRUEL PRANKS
Draco enjoys taunting those he regards as inferior. He flies off with Neville's Remembrall to put it on the roof, out of poor Neville's reach.

NEVILLE LONGBOTTOM
FORGETFUL FIRST-YEAR

Poor, nervous Neville often has a worried expression

NEVILLE IS
a shy, slightly awkward first-year who despite being afraid of many things and people, displays moments of great courage and spirit. He even stands up to his friends Harry, Ron, and Hermione when they try to break school rules.

REMEMBRALL
This clear minifigure head piece is a Remembrall—a magical object which glows red when you've forgotten something. The trouble is, Neville can't remember what it is that he's forgotten.

Wrist gets broken in his first flying lesson

Neville has a broom, but he struggles to control it

MEMORY JOGGER
Neville's gran sends him a Remembrall because he's always forgetting things. In this LEGO set, clumsy Neville forgets to look where he's going and is about to fall off.

MAGICAL FILE

YEAR: 2021
SET: 76395: Hogwarts: First Flying Lesson
ACCESSORIES: Broom, Remembrall, wand

SUSAN BONES
HUFFLEPUFF STUDENT

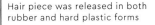

Hair piece was released in both rubber and hard plastic forms

MAGICAL FILE

YEAR: 2018

SET: 75954: Hogwarts Great Hall

ACCESSORIES: Broomstick, mug

Freckled face print is shared with Ginny Weasley

The first appearance of the LEGO Hufflepuff black-and-yellow torso piece

SUSAN BONES is the first Hufflepuff student to have a minifigure, but not the last. She joins Hogwarts in the same year as Harry Potter and travels across the Great Lake from Hogsmeade station in a self-propelled boat with Hermione and Seamus.

OLDER AND WISER
In the 2023 Hufflepuff™ House Banner set (76412), Susan is older. With longer legs and a more mature face print, she wears her hair in the same style as Moaning Myrtle.

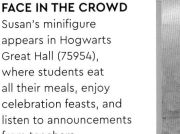

FACE IN THE CROWD
Susan's minifigure appears in Hogwarts Great Hall (75954), where students eat all their meals, enjoy celebration feasts, and listen to announcements from teachers.

FILIUS FLITWICK
CHARMING PROFESSOR

In Harry's first year, Flitwick has a bald patch and a bushy white beard

PART-GOBLIN, PART-WIZARD, Filius Flitwick is Professor of Charms, head of Ravenclaw house, and former dueling champion. Kind and cheerful, he exudes enthusiasm for Charms and teaching, and he's been doing it a long time— Flitwick even taught Professor Snape.

Wand used for competitive dueling

Short, unarticulated leg piece used for goblin and house-elf minifigures

MAGICAL FILE

YEAR: 2021

SETS: 76385: Hogwarts Moment: Charms Class

ACCESSORIES: Wand

DID YOU KNOW?

Flitwick's minifigures reflect his two very different appearances between the first two films and the later ones (see page 129).

SMALL BUT MIGHTY
Professor Flitwick stands on a stack of books to be seen, but he has a good command of his classroom and is well respected by staff and students.

HARRY POTTER

GRYFFINDOR SEEKER

PLAYING BALL

Hogwarts Quidditch matches always draw big crowds. As Gryffindor Seeker, Harry ends the game and wins 150 points when he catches the tiny, winged ball called the Golden Snitch.

MAGICAL FILE

YEAR: 2018
SETS: 75956: Quidditch Match
ACCESSORIES: Broom, Golden Snitch

Alternate face has a startled expression. Perhaps because in his first match, Harry catches the Snitch in his mouth

Harry is the only minifigure in the team with short legs because he is the youngest Seeker in a century

QUIDDITCH CUP

Through the year, all four Hogwarts houses compete for the highly contested Quidditch Cup. Gryffindor and Slytherin have a particular rivalry.

DESPITE HAVING NEVER flown a broom before, Harry takes to it faster than you can say "Quidditch"—a sport played on brooms with seven players and three types of ball. He is such a natural that he's chosen to join the Gryffindor Quidditch team in his first year.

29

OLIVER WOOD
GRYFFINDOR QUIDDITCH CAPTAIN

Oliver's team finally wins the Quidditch Cup in his last year at school

OLIVER WOOD is the Gryffindor Quidditch captain and is determined to win. He pushes his team hard in the hope of making them as driven and focused as he is. He leads them in inter-house matches in their house colors of scarlet and gold.

DID YOU KNOW?
Oliver Wood finishes school at the end of Harry's third year, but he returns four years later to fight in the Battle of Hogwarts.

Full-size legs because Oliver is four years older than Harry

HE'S A KEEPER
As well as being captain, Oliver plays in the position of Keeper. He guards his team's three hoops to prevent the other team scoring goals with the Quaffle.

MAGICAL FILE

YEAR: 2018

SETS: 75956: Quidditch Match

ACCESSORIES: Broom

MARCUS FLINT
SLYTHERIN QUIDDITCH CAPTAIN

Crooked teeth are visible when he jeers at the opposition

QUIDDITCH CAN BE a brutal game, but that's particularly true when Slytherins are playing. Marcus Flint, captain of Slytherin, is a fast and agile flier, but his aggressive bullying sets the tone for his team's cut-throat play and bad sportsmanship.

MAGICAL FILE

YEAR: 2018

SETS: 75956: Quidditch Match

ACCESSORIES: Broom

Torso piece has a printed hood on the back with silver edging

Brown Quidditch gloves give grip and protection

DID YOU KNOW?
Marcus's LEGO broom has a stud-shooter attached to it so he can fire the Quaffle at the goal hoops.

GOAL-ORIENTED
As one of three Chasers, Flint plays the Quaffle across the pitch and tries to get it past the Keeper and through one of their three hoops to score ten points for each goal.

LUCIAN BOLE

SLYTHERIN BEATER

Hair piece is shared with Seamus Finnigan

Beater's bat is made from a telescope element and the piece used for Mad-Eye Moody's Polyjuice bottle

Face looks complacent on one side and is wailing like a bad loser on the other

DID YOU KNOW?

When Lucian Bole leaves Hogwarts, the two new Beaters on the team are Draco Malfoy's burly sidekicks Vincent Crabbe and Gregory Goyle.

MAGICAL FILE

YEAR: 2018

SET: 75956: Quidditch Match

ACCESSORIES: Broom, Beater's bat

FOUL PLAY

The Quidditch set includes the scoreboard from the highly contested Slytherin-Gryffindor match. Lucian does whatever he can to keep it in Slytherin's favor.

LUCIAN BOLE is a Slytherin Quidditch player who wants to beat the other Houses' players—both in the game and with his Beater's bat. As a beater, it's his job to whack the heavy Bludger balls at the opposition to throw them off their game.

DEAN THOMAS
GRYFFINDOR CLASSMATE

Unique Gryffindor tile with clips

MAGICAL FILE

YEAR: 2018
SET: 71022: LEGO Harry Potter Minifigures Series 1
ACCESSORIES: Gryffindor flag

Long, printed Gryffindor scarf for watching chilly winter Quidditch matches

A BIG SPORTS FAN, Dean Thomas supports the Muggle soccer team West Ham as well as turning out to cheer on his Quidditch team. He later plays for the Gryffindor team himself as a Chaser.

WINTER WARMER
A medium-legged Dean wraps up warmly in cozy clothes to venture out to Hogsmeade in a 2021 set.

TRUE FRIEND
Always a loyal friend to Harry, Dean enjoys a frothy, refreshing Butterbeer with him in the Three Broomsticks in Hogsmeade Village Visit (set 76388).

ANGELINA JOHNSON
QUIDDITCH STAR

BEING TWO YEARS OLDER than Harry, Angelina is in the same year as Fred and George Weasley. Like them, she's a keen Quidditch player. She plays as Chaser for the Gryffindor team and then rises to captain after Oliver Wood.

Raised eyebrow—as team captain, Angelina takes no nonsense

DID YOU KNOW?
Along with Angelina, the Gryffindor common room set includes Quidditch gear: a broom, a Golden Snitch, and an energy-giving chocolate bar.

Longer leg piece fits perfectly in the red common room armchair

New 2023 style of ribbed Quidditch sweater instead of earlier draw-string robes

HEAD IN THE GAME
Angelina takes Quidditch very seriously. In the 2023 Gryffindor™ House Banner set (76409), she plans her strategies and meets with fellow players in the cozy Gryffindor Common Room.

MAGICAL FILE

YEAR: 2023

SET: 76409: Gryffindor™ House Banner

ACCESSORIES: Wand, broom

HARRY POTTER

HAVE A VERY HARRY CHRISTMAS

CHRISTMAS AT SCHOOL MAY SEEM as unappealing as a double detention with Snape, but Harry loves it. Unlike at the Dursleys', he's surrounded by friends, can enjoy himself, and also receives nice presents.

MAGICAL FILE

YEAR: 2019

SET: 75964: Harry Potter Advent Calendar (2019)

ACCESSORIES: Goblet, wand

Festive minifigure was an exclusive with the first Advent Calendar set

Woolly sweater is a present knitted by Mrs. Weasley

Casual trousers are worn at school during the holidays

R IS FOR RON

The Weasleys can't afford extravagant gifts, but Ron's mom shows her love by knitting personalized sweaters for all the family.

THE MAGIC OF CHRISTMAS

In the first LEGO Harry Potter Advent Calendar, Harry gets to enjoy the festive celebrations with enchanted decorations and snow-covered pine trees from the Hogwarts grounds.

HARRY POTTER
THE INVISIBLE BOY

AT CHRISTMAS, Harry receives a magical present from a mysterious person. The Invisibility Cloak is one of the three Deathly Hallows—legendary objects of great power. It belonged to Harry's father, and Dumbledore passes it on to Harry anonymously.

WALKING FREE

The new Invisibility Cloak is just what Harry needs for sneaking around after curfew. The caretaker Filch and his cat might be suspicious, but if they can't see Harry, they can't catch him.

Pajama printing because Harry goes to the Restricted Section of the library at night

Holographic fabric

Inside of cloak has a printed pattern

MAGICAL FILE

YEAR: 2018

SET: 71022: LEGO Harry Potter Minifigures Series 1

ACCESSORIES: Invisibility cloak

HIDDEN HARRY

Harry can also be seen (or not...) with his cloak in Hogwarts: Dumbledore's Office (76402), though he wears his robes rather than pajamas.

JAMES POTTER

HARRY'S DAD

Same style glasses as Harry

Printed sideburns join with hair piece

People comment on how James and Harry look alike

MAGICAL FILE

YEAR: 2020

SET: 71028: LEGO Harry Potter Minifigures Series 2

ACCESSORIES: Family portrait

LIKE HARRY, James Potter was a Gryffindor and a Quidditch player. But he was killed by Voldemort when Harry was just a baby. James's group of friends, called the Marauders, were James, Sirius Black, Remus Lupin, and Peter Pettigrew.

Unique, removable scarf piece

MIRROR OF ERISED
The Mirror of Erised ("desire" backward) shows your strongest desires, so Harry sees his parents. The LEGO model has removable panels, depending on which minifigure is looking at it.

PICTURE PERFECT
Photographs, along with the mirror and people's memories, are the only ways Harry knows what his parents looked like.

LILY POTTER

HARRY'S MOM

FAMILY TIES

When Voldemort attacked the Potter family, Harry's mom, Lily, sacrificed herself to protect her baby. This act of love gave Harry magical protection that lasted beyond that moment.

People say Harry has Lily's eyes

LILY EVANS was Muggle-born, and became a talented witch who joined Gryffindor House. She ended up marrying James Potter, but when she was younger she was friends with his rival, Severus Snape.

Printed black shoes

DID YOU KNOW?

Baby Harry has the same LEGO mold as the tiny, diminished form of He Who Must Not Be Named in The Rise of Voldemort (75965) (p.132).

MAGICAL FILE

YEAR: 2020

SET: 71028: LEGO Harry Potter Minifigures Series 2

ACCESSORIES: Baby Harry

IRMA PINCE
HOGWARTS LIBRARIAN

Unique witch's hat piece with detachable feather

WOE BETIDE anyone caught treating a book badly in the school library. Madam Pince, the strict librarian, places a higher value on her books than on the students. Her stern minifigure is very protective of her tomes and will not stand for any disrespect.

MINE OF INFORMATION
Madam Pince helps students looking for suitable information, such as studious Hermione, but she is fierce to anyone who breaks the library rules.

Wide band of green edging on gown

MAGICAL FILE

YEAR: 2022
SET: 76402: Hogwarts: Dumbledore's Office
ACCESSORIES: Wand, book

HARRY POTTER

FEARLESS FIRST-YEAR

DESPITE A SERIES of protective spells and obstacles, the Sorcerer's Stone isn't safe. Harry, Ron, and Hermione set out on a mission to stop Voldemort from snatching it. If Voldemort used it to make the Elixir of Life, he could be restored to full, deadly strength.

MAGICAL FILE

YEAR: 2021
SET: 76392: Hogwarts Wizard's Chess
ACCESSORIES: Wand

Reverse side of face looks terrified by the challenges that lie in wait

Sweater is ripped during dangerous task to reach the Sorcerer's Stone

Corduroy pants

BLUNT INSTRUMENT
The trick to sneaking past the ferocious guard dog, Fluffy, is to play some music. A tune from an enchanted harp will send him straight to sleep.

THREE-HEADED TROUBLE
He might not look very Fluffy, but that's the name of the vicious three-headed dog that Hagrid sets to guard the Sorcerer's Stone. He stands on the trapdoor in the out-of-bounds third-floor corridor (76387).

HERMIONE GRANGER
QUICK-WITTED

WHEN HERMIONE, Harry, and Ron go after the Sorcerer's Stone, Hermione's cool head and bright ideas save them from being strangled by a Devil's Snare. The more you struggle, the tighter the plant will grip you with its tentacles.

All the younger Hermione minifigures have this frizzy hair piece with bangs

Though calm here, the other side of her head looks very alarmed

STEP BY STEP
Hermione, Harry, and Ron can only cross the chessboard and reach their destination by playing their way across it. One wrong step and they will be blocked—or maybe even worse.

MAGICAL FILE

YEAR: 2021
SET: 76392: Hogwarts Wizard's Chess
ACCESSORIES: Wand

Unique torso piece

DID YOU KNOW?
The Sorcerer's Stone is a legendary substance created by Nicolas Flamel. It turns metal into gold and produces the Elixir of Life, which bestows immortality.

RON WEASLEY
WIZARD CHESS PLAYER

Bashful expression hides Ron's genius chess skills

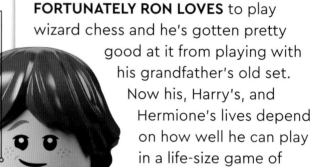

FORTUNATELY RON LOVES to play wizard chess and he's gotten pretty good at it from playing with his grandfather's old set. Now his, Harry's, and Hermione's lives depend on how well he can play in a life-size game of enchanted pieces.

KNIGHT IN SHINING ARMOR

Each player takes a spot on the board. Ron plays as a knight, expertly directing his friends—until he is toppled in an act of self-sacrifice. It's the only way they can win and Harry can go on to the next room.

Only this minifigure has this torso piece

MAGICAL FILE

YEAR: 2021
SET: 76392: Hogwarts Wizard's Chess
ACCESSORIES: Wand

Ron ends up in the hospital wing after his round of wizard chess

SMASHING GAME

Wizard chess is barbaric: when one piece defeats another, it smashes it to pieces. These LEGO playing pieces can also be taken apart and then put back together for the next game.

QUIRINUS QUIRRELL
POWERLESS PROFESSOR

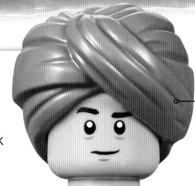

PROFESSOR QUIRRELL is the new teacher for Defense Against the Dark Arts, but he's hiding a dark secret. He dangerously underestimates his ability to control Voldemort, and the Dark Lord attaches himself to the back of Quirrell's head.

Lavender headdress was acquired on travels to a distant land

MAGICAL FILE

YEAR: 2018
SET: 75954: Hogwarts Great Hall
ACCESSORIES: Wand

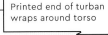

Printed end of turban wraps around torso

SURRENDER TO THE DARK ARTS
Voldemort is desperate to get the Sorcerer's Stone because it can restore him to strength. He uses Quirrell to get past the obstacles guarding it.

HATS OFF
Hidden under Quirrell's turban, on the other side of his head, is the terrible truth—a printing of Voldemort's barely human face.

CHAPTER TWO

HARRY POTTER AND THE CHAMBER OF SECRETS™

OLLIVANDERS
WAND SHOP

SCRIBBULUS
STATIONERS

THE WAND
CHOOSES THE
WIZARD.

BUSTLING DIAGON ALLEY is the place to stock up on essentials for the new school year, from wands in Ollivanders to a brand-new broom in Quality Quidditch Supplies. Before Harry's second year, there's extra excitement in the air because of a celebrity book signing at Flourish & Blotts.

FLOREAN FORTESCUE'S ICE-CREAM PARLOR

FLOURISH & BLOTTS

QUALITY QUIDDITCH SUPPLIES

NICE BIG SMILE, HARRY. TOGETHER, YOU AND I RATE THE FRONT PAGE.

HARRY POTTER

SECOND-YEAR GRYFFINDOR

MANY PEOPLE long for the summer break, but for Harry, that's when he has to go back to the disagreeable Dursleys. They are fearful of him and don't understand his power. But they also don't realize he isn't allowed to do magic outside school.

MAGICAL FILE

YEAR: 2020
SET: 75968: 4 Privet Drive
ACCESSORIES: Wand, suitcase, Hedwig

Wand terrifies the Dursleys

Harry now has his own clothes that fit

Casual clothes don't draw suspicion in the Surrey village of Little Whinging

BACK TO HOGWARTS

Harry wears the same clothes in Hogwarts Whomping Willow (75953) and Hogwarts Gryffindor Dorms (40452), except he has gray instead of black trousers.

WEASLEYS TO THE RESCUE!

When Uncle Vernon forbids Harry from returning to Hogwarts, Ron arrives in his dad's enchanted flying car to pull the bars off Harry's window and whisk him away from Privet Drive.

VERNON DURSLEY
HARRY'S HORRIBLE UNCLE

Hands often express Vernon's anger when he loses his temper

Minifigure's two expressions are cross and self-satisfied

HOME SWEET HOME
Proud Vernon and Petunia live in a very ordinary house in a very ordinary street with their son, Dudley. Their worst fear is that the neighbors might think they are in any way strange.

THE DURSLEYS ARE the worst type of Muggles imaginable, but they're the only family Harry has. Uncle Vernon is narrow-minded and self-important. When he took Harry in, he swore that he'd put an end to all that magical nonsense.

Plain, beige clothes appeal to this very unadventurous Dursley

MAGICAL FILE

YEAR: 2020
SET: 75968: 4 Privet Drive
ACCESSORIES: None

DID YOU KNOW?
Vernon made Harry sleep in the cupboard under the stairs until he was shamed into reluctantly giving Dudley's second bedroom to Harry.

PETUNIA DURSLEY

HARRY'S CRUEL AUNT

MAGICAL FILE

YEAR: 2020
SET: 75968: 4 Privet Drive
ACCESSORIES: Cake

Minifigure's two expressions are sour and horrified

Petunia favors floral patterns and other feminine styles

AUNT PETUNIA IS deeply concerned with appearances. She presents herself as prim and proper, but is very unpleasant. Exceedingly house proud, she runs a shipshape household, but she spoils her "Duddykins" and treats Harry with contempt.

FUNNY BUSINESS

Petunia bakes an elaborate cake to impress influential business contacts. But Dobby the house-elf floats it onto a guest's head to get Harry into trouble in an attempt to prevent him from returning to Hogwarts.

DID YOU KNOW?

Young Petunia Evans grew to resent her sister Lily's magical powers. Her bitterness poisoned their relationship like Venomous Tentacula.

DUDLEY DURSLEY
HARRY'S BULLY COUSIN

Dudley's hair has a side part, like his father's

MAGICAL FILE

YEAR: 2020
SET: 75968: 4 Privet Drive
ACCESSORIES: None

Argyle sweater and collared shirt are a mini version of his father's taste in clothes

DUDLEY DURSLEY and Harry grow up together in the same house, but Dudley has a very different experience. His parents teach him from a very young age that he is special and far more important than his orphaned cousin.

Printed stomach bulge

PAJAMAS AND PIG TAILS
Dudley's 2021 Advent Calendar minifigure has a corkscrew pig tail poking out of his striped pajamas—a "gift" from Hagrid for scoffing Harry's birthday cake.

RULING THE ROOST
Spoiled rotten, Dudley calls the shots because he's been pampered and indulged. He's used to getting what he wants with tantrums and aggression.

DOBBY
COURAGEOUS HOUSE-ELF

HOUSE-ELVES ARE SECOND-CLASS citizens who have to serve their masters, and Dobby is bound to the despicable Malfoy family. Dobby warns Harry that he's in danger and tries to save him—albeit by turning his life upside down and getting him into trouble.

Tatty pillowcase is all Dobby has to wear

MAGICAL FILE

YEAR: 2018
SET: 71022: LEGO® Harry Potter Minifigures Series 1
ACCESSORIES: Tom Riddle's diary, sock

Sock is a symbol of Dobby's freedom from the Malfoys

Book cover has a mark from when the Horcrux within it was destroyed

UNINVITED GUEST
While Harry's aunt and uncle are entertaining, Harry is meant to be in his room, being quiet, and pretending he doesn't exist. It's really not a convenient time for a noisy house-elf to appear.

FRESH FACED
In 4 Privet Drive (75968) in 2020, Dobby has the same mold, but an updated face print with an open-mouthed smile and bolder eyes.

MR. BORGIN
SHADY SHOPKEEPER

Printed brown and gray sideburns merge with hair piece

Scar under right eye

DID YOU KNOW?

Like his minifigure, Mr. Borgin is two-faced. He panders to customers to flatter them into spending money, but behind their backs, he's contemptuous of them.

ONE OF THE OWNERS of Borgin and Burkes, Mr. Borgin takes an unhealthy interest in the Dark Arts and dangerous magical artifacts. He revels in collecting them for his shop, buying from and selling to people who are mostly up to no good.

Neat, respectable suit for disreputable salesman

MAGICAL FILE

YEAR: 2021

SET: 40500: Wizarding World Minifigure Accessory Set

ACCESSORIES: Wand

KNOCKTURN ALLEY
Borgin and Burkes is just off Diagon Alley. Harry lands there after a Floo powder mishap. Hagrid whisks him away—it's not the sort of place a young wizard should hang about.

MOLLY WEASLEY
KIND-HEARTED MATRIARCH

Caring Molly has two face prints, and both are smiling

Furry purple collar adds to Molly's mish-mash style of second-hand clothes

MOLLY WEASLEY is a talented witch who fights for what's right. Mother to a boisterous brood of seven, she also takes Harry under her wing. Every summer, she takes everyone to stock up on school essentials in Diagon Alley.

MAGICAL FILE

YEAR: 2020
SET: 75978: Diagon Alley
ACCESSORIES: None

Arms are quick to welcome Harry into the family

DID YOU KNOW?

Molly, like her husband Arthur, is a pure-blood wizard. However, this doesn't affect their view that everyone—witch, wizard, or Muggle— is equal.

SHOPPING SPREE
There's excitement in the air on this trip because celebrity wizard Gilderoy Lockhart is signing copies of his new book! Molly is a big fan—but then, she's never actually met him.

HERMIONE GRANGER
THE BRIGHTEST WITCH IN HER YEAR

Second-year Hermione minifigures still have the bushy hair piece with thick bangs

OPEN BOOK
Hermione is excited to read Gilderoy Lockhart's new autobiography, *Magical Me*. It's in its 27th week as a *Daily Prophet* best-seller. The LEGO book hinges open to reveal a tile piece.

HERMIONE EXCELLED in her first year—both in exams and in the practical application of magic to defeat Voldemort. Now she can't wait to get her books and supplies from Diagon Alley and get started on her second year. There's so much to learn!

Torso print is different from other cloaked ones—it's closed at the bottom and there's no tie at the top

Casual clothes are worn under Gryffindor cloak for shopping

MAGICAL FILE

YEAR: 2020

SET: 75978: Diagon Alley

ACCESSORIES: Quill, Fred Weasley's Basic Blaze Box

THE PEN IS MIGHTIER THAN THE WAND
Scribbulus Writing Implements on Diagon Alley smells of fresh parchment, new quills, and ink. It's an essential stop for Hermione to stock up on stationery— she gets through a lot of it!

GILDEROY LOCKHART
CELEBRITY CHARLATAN

GILDEROY LOCKHART HAS built a gilded career with his self-promotion, luscious hair, winning smile, and use of Memory Charms to claim other wizards' brave exploits as his own. Now he's headed to Hogwarts as Professor of Defense Against the Dark Arts.

The other side of his face has beads of sweat for when he has to deliver on his reputation

Smile has won *Witch Weekly's* Most Charming Smile award five times

MAGICAL FILE

YEAR: 2020

SET: 75978: Diagon Alley

ACCESSORIES: Quill

Gold waistcoat is printed with metallic ink

Two-tone cape is violet on the outside and yellow on the inside

DRESSED TO IMPRESS
Lockhart likes to make an impression with his many flamboyant, colorful outfits. His minifigure from 2021 wears head-to-toe golden yellow.

SEEKING THE LIMELIGHT
Lockhart courts the press wherever he goes. He can't resist having his photo taken by the *Daily Prophet* photographer with the famous Boy Who Lived, Harry Potter.

FLOREAN FORTESCUE
PURVEYOR OF FINE ICE CREAM

Same receding hair piece as Ollivander and Nearly Headless Nick, but this color is unique to this minifigure

MAGICAL FILE

YEAR: 2020
SET: 75978: Diagon Alley
ACCESSORIES: Ice cream scoop, ice cream

SWEET SPOT
A trip to Diagon Alley is a sad one without a visit to the ice cream parlor in all its knickerbocker glory. Harry and Ron pop in to see friendly old Florean and buy delicious sundaes.

Ice-cream-wafer-inspired pattern on waistcoat

Chocolate and caramel colored trousers and shirt

SAVOR THE FLAVORS
Fortescue's has more flavors than you can wave a wand at. From chocolate with peanut butter to black beer and raisin or bat juice and earwig, there really is something for everyone.

FOR THE SCOOP ON where to go for the best ice cream, head to Florean Fortescue's Ice Cream Parlor in Diagon Alley. This wizard knows a thing or two about ice cream.

WITCH
MAGICAL CUSTOMER

THIS WITCH is on a shopping spree, but she doesn't look very happy. Diagon Alley has the best collection of quality stores, but it gets very crowded before the start of the school year—when everyone rushes there to stock up on their supplies list.

Bent witch's hat and hair piece is shared with Professor Sinistra

The same sour, unimpressed expression as Aunt Petunia

Money bags for Galleons, Sickles, and Knuts

MYSTERY CUSTOMER
A rather dapper minifigure is also shopping in the Wizarding World Accessory set (40500). It looks like he gets his suit torsos from the same place as the Mr. Ollivander and Griphook minifigures.

WHAT'S IN STORE?
Diagon Alley sells the best the wizarding world has to offer: pewter and iron cauldrons, live owls, potion ingredients, and tasty treats such as acid pops.

MAGICAL FILE

YEAR: 2021
SET: 40500: Wizarding World Accessory Set
ACCESSORIES: None

LUCIUS MALFOY
DEATH EATER

Lucius shares Dumbledore's hair piece, but in yellow, which is unique to this minifigure

MAGICAL FILE

YEAR: 2020
SET: 75978: Diagon Alley
ACCESSORIES: Cane

Serpentine clasp

Malfoy carries a cane, which conceals his wand

IF YOU EVER wondered where Draco gets his arrogance, privilege, and ideas about pure-blood superiority, look no further than his father. Lucius Malfoy comes from a long line of self-serving, rich wizards, and he secretly serves the Dark Lord.

Leg print is shared with other minifigures, but the tops of their jackets are all different

EVIL INTENT
The diary of Tom Riddle is a harmful magical object. Trouble starts when Lucius Malfoy slips it in with Ginny's shopping at Flourish and Blott's.

BULLYING ROLE MODEL
Haughty Lucius and Draco sweep through the shops to make their purchases, but they don't mix with all the ordinary folk there. Except to insult them to their minifigure faces.

RON WEASLEY
LATE FOR SCHOOL

RON'S MINIFIGURE in tan-and-brown clothes is dressed for action. He rescues Harry from Privet Drive, flies a car, is thrashed by the Whomping Willow, and then finally relaxes in the Gryffindor dormitory after a stern lecture from teachers.

All the younger Ron minifigures have this dark-orange hair piece

Alternative face is frozen in terror

Ribbed sweater pattern continues on the back of the torso

OUT ON A LIMB

Ron and Harry fly Mr. Weasley's enchanted Ford Anglia to Hogwarts when their access to the Hogwarts Express is mysteriously closed. They end up crashing into the vicious Whomping Willow.

TALKING SHOP

Ron wears a Gryffindor cloak over simple jeans when he goes shopping in Diagon Alley (75978).

MAGICAL FILE

YEAR: 2018

SETS: 75953: Hogwarts Whomping Willow (2018); 75968: 4 Privet Drive (2020); 40452: Hogwarts Gryffindor Dorms (2021)

ACCESSORIES: Wand, chocolate frog

ALBUS DUMBLEDORE
HEADMASTER IN PERIL

Dumbledore's minifigures change outfits, but the twinkle in his eye behind his half-moon specs always remains

MAGICAL FILE

YEAR: 2021

SET: 76389: Hogwarts: Chamber of Secrets

ACCESSORIES: None

HARRY'S SECOND YEAR
starts well, but horrors soon start unfolding. A deadly threat hangs over the school, and forces are conspiring against the headmaster. Calm Dumbledore keeps his head, but can he keep his school and students safe?

This white beard piece features on five Dumbledore minifigures

Curved sloped skirt piece instead of legs for long robes

TICKLED PINK
Also in Magenta robes, a 2022 minifigure of Dumbledore towers over a mini set of Hogwarts castle that can be built in many different ways.

AS WISE AS AN OWL
Dumbledore addresses the Great Hall from behind his elegant lectern that is carved like a bird with outstretched wings. The LEGO owl piece was designed for this set, and it stands on a goblet.

POMONA SPROUT

HERBOLOGY PROFESSOR

Hat is smaller than McGonagall's and looks like a plant shoot

JOLLY PROFESSOR

Pomona Sprout is head of Hufflepuff house and she teaches Herbology—the study of magical plants. Her greenhouse is also a working garden, where she grows vital medicine, such as Mandrake juice for reversing petrification.

MAGICAL FILE

YEAR: 2021

SETS: 76384: Hogwarts Moment: Herbology Class

ACCESSORIES: Wand, scissors

Dirt marks on coveralls

Dual-molded leg piece has boots for muddy work

EARLY SPROUT

In 2020, the first Professor Sprout minifigure sported the same hat but had a sloped skirt piece rather than trousers and boots.

GREEN FINGERS

Professor Sprout potters in her greenhouse, tending her pumpkin patch with a pair of scissors, a shovel, buckets, a watering station, and plant pots.

CEDRIC DIGGORY
HERBOLOGY STUDENT

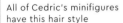
All of Cedric's minifigures have this hair style

MAGICAL FILE

YEAR: 2021

SETS: 76384: Hogwarts Moment: Herbology Class

ACCESSORIES: Plant, bucket

DASHING CEDRIC DIGGORY is a Hufflepuff student who is two years older than Harry. All students, including this minifigure, study Herbology. Despite the anonymous coveralls, Cedric's face print and hair piece make him very recognizable.

Sand-yellow removable ear defenders are unique to this set

Protective coveralls worn for gardening

Legs are longer than Neville's because Cedric is older

GARDENING LEAVE
In the Hufflepuff™ House Banner set (76412), green-fingered Cedric works on tending flowers and plants in the sunny Hufflepuff common room in his 2023 Quidditch wear.

CALL OF THE WILD
Today's practical Herbology lesson is repotting baby Mandrakes. Ear defenders are essential because the Mandrake's cry can be deadly. Even these seedling's wails can knock you out.

NEVILLE LONGBOTTOM
EAGER HERBOLOGIST

Ear defenders molded with hair piece

Concerned expression—the other side shows Neville's fainting eyes closed

Gryffindor tie under protective coveralls

THINGS OFTEN SEEM TO GO WRONG for clumsy Neville, and he doesn't think he's any good at anything. Lessons never seem to go his way, but Professor Sprout spots that he shows real aptitude for Herbology.

MAGICAL FILE

YEAR: 2018
SET: 71022: LEGO Harry Potter Minifigures Series 1
ACCESSORIES: Wand, Mandrake plant

ALL EARS
In 2021, Neville's minifigure takes greater risks with the Mandrakes—his ear defenders are around his neck rather than attached to his head.

GONE TO POT
Even with ear defenders, poor old Neville still succumbs to the sound of the powerful Mandrake plants. He faints and spends the lesson lying on the floor.

DRACO MALFOY
SLYTHERIN SEEKER

DRACO MALFOY is used to getting whatever he wants. In his second year, he makes the Slytherin Quidditch team, but only after his dad buys the rest of the team top-of-the-range Nimbus 2001 brooms. Like his fellow players, Draco bullies his way around the pitch.

GOING FOR GOLD
The molded Golden Snitch, which clips into a minifigure's hand, first appeared with Draco's standalone minifigure in 2018 and later in Quidditch Match (75956).

Shorter cape than Draco's older teammates Flint and Bole have

Same torso piece as other Slytherin players

Printed drawstrings for cape

MAGICAL FILE

YEAR: 2018

SET: 71022: LEGO Harry Potter Minifigures Series 1

ACCESSORIES: Green broom, golden snitch, wand

ALL SET
Between matches, Quidditch balls need restraining in a box so they don't fly away. A full set includes two Beaters' bats and four balls: a Quaffle, two Bludgers and the Golden Snitch.

MOANING MYRTLE
GLOOMY GHOST

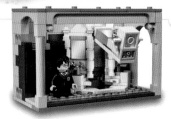

SINK HOLE
In the girls' bathroom Harry finds the opening to the Chamber of Secrets—the home of the yellow-eyed monster. Myrtle tells Harry that if he dies down there, he can share the bathroom.

Alternate face is crying and has a tear on her cheek

FIFTY YEARS AGO, distraught student Myrtle was crying in the toilets after being teased about her glasses. Then she heard a noise, saw a pair of great big yellow eyes... and died instantly. Her moping ghost now haunts the girls' bathroom.

Foot comes with a transparent angled support so Myrtle looks like she's floating

Tom Riddle's diary hits Myrtle when Ginny throws it down the toilet

LOOKING A LOT LIKE CHRISTMAS
Myrtle's 2022 Advent Calendar variant is less blue—both in coloring and in mood. The black-white-and-gray ghost is even smiling a little. Well, it is the season to be jolly.

MAGICAL FILE

YEARS: 2020

SET: 71028: LEGO Harry Potter Minifigures Series 2

ACCESSORIES: Tom Riddle's diary

HARRY POTTER
GREGORY GOYLE IMPERSONATOR

Determined face—will the audacious plan work?

Alternate face print looks like Gregory Goyle's clueless face

MAGICAL FILE

YEARS: 2022

SET: 76386: Hogwarts Polyjuice Potion Mistake

ACCESSORIES: Goyle's hair piece, wand, goblet of potion

Slytherin torso matches all three minifigures in this set

HARRY, RON, AND HERMIONE are convinced that Draco knows something about who has opened the Chamber of Secrets. Maybe he is the Heir of Slytherin? The only way to get Draco to talk is for Ron and Harry to pose as Crabbe and Goyle.

GREGORY GOYLE
Harry's minifigure comes with an alternate face printing and a separate hair piece to make a full figure of Goyle.

POLYJUICE POTION
Polyjuice Potion allows the drinker to transform temporarily into the form of another person. Hermione has never seen a more complicated recipe, but if anyone can make it, she can.

RON WEASLEY
VINCENT CRABBE IMPERSONATOR

Ron pulls this face when he tastes the disgusting Polyjuice Potion

Ron's ginger hair is the first thing to come back when the potion begins to wear off

Alternate face print looks like Vincent Crabbe's

WITH THEIR BODIES transformed into Draco's two sidekicks with Polyjuice Potion, Ron and Harry hightail it to the Slytherin common room in the dungeons. They ask Draco about the Chamber of Secrets, but he doesn't know much.

CLOAKROOM AND DAGGER
They secretly make the Polyjuice Potion in one of the girls' bathrooms. No one ever goes in because of Moaning Myrtle—the ghost who wails and shouts at everyone.

VINCENT CRABBE
Ron's minifigure comes with an alternate face printing and a separate hair piece to make a full figure of Crabbe.

MAGICAL FILE

YEAR: 2022

SET: 76386: Hogwarts Polyjuice Potion Mistake

ACCESSORIES: Crabbe's hair piece, wand, goblet of potion

HERMIONE GRANGER

CAT PERSON

Back of cat face is shaped just like Hermione's wavy hair

Unique cat mask fits over Hermione's head piece

MAGICAL FILE

YEAR: 2022

SET: 76386: Hogwarts Polyjuice Potion Mistake

ACCESSORIES: Hair piece, wand, goblet of potion

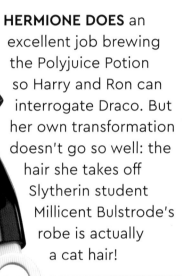

Same Slytherin torso as worn by real Slytherins

HERMIONE DOES an excellent job brewing the Polyjuice Potion so Harry and Ron can interrogate Draco. But her own transformation doesn't go so well: the hair she takes off Slytherin student Millicent Bulstrode's robe is actually a cat hair!

READY FOR ACTION

Before she drinks the potion, Hermione's regular head and hair style are paired with Slytherin robes, to fully impersonate Millicent Bulstrode.

SICK AS A DOG

Mortified Hermione doesn't want to leave the toilet cubicle, but eventually she has to face the music. It takes a few days but she makes a full recovery thanks to Madam Pomfrey.

PANSY PARKINSON
SNEERING SLYTHERIN

Hair style with face-framing tendrils and ponytail is similar to Hannah Abbott's

Self-satisfied smirk

First Slytherin torso to feature a cardigan

TAUNTS, JIBES, AND CRUEL comments are what most of Pansy's classmates get from her. She particularly dislikes Harry and his group—but she's also quick to mock her own friends, who appear to look up to her as their leader.

DID YOU KNOW?
Pansy Parkinson is the first female Slytherin minifigure. The only other girl to wear LEGO Slytherin robes is Hermione when she tries to impersonate Millicent Bulstrode.

CHARM SCHOOL
Down in the dungeons is the Slytherin Common Room. It's not a warm, welcoming place for non-Slytherins, and Pansy does her wizarding homework here while enjoying Draco's company.

MAGICAL FILE
YEAR: 2023
SET: 76410: Slytherin™ House Banner
ACCESSORIES: Wand, broom

AURORA SINISTRA
ASTRONOMY PROFESSOR

Crooked hat and hair are a single piece

Alternative face print wears glasses

IF IT'S WRITTEN in the stars, then Professor Sinistra can find it. She teaches Astronomy—chronicling the movements of the stars, planets, and other celestial bodies. Her lessons often take place at night, but there's no sleeping in class!

DID YOU KNOW?

The main LEGO piece that Professor Sinistra's telescope is built with was first created in 1994 as a video camera.

Gold metallic printing

MAGICAL FILE

YEAR: 2021

SET: 76389: Hogwarts Chamber of Secrets

ACCESSORIES: Wand, telescope

GUIDING STAR

Professor Sinistra teaches many of her lessons at the top of the Astronomy Tower. Students look through telescopes and fill in star charts.

69

SEAMUS FINNIGAN
IRISH GRYFFINDOR

Both Seamus's minifigures have this hair piece, as does Lucian Bole's

MAGICAL FILE

YEAR: 2021
SET: 76383: Hogwarts Moment: Potions Class
ACCESSORIES: Wand, book with potion tile

WITH A MUGGLE FATHER and a witch mother, half-blood Seamus is comfortable in both the Muggle and the wizarding worlds. The chatty Gryffindor has Irish roots and is best friends with Dean Thomas. He's not shy, often asking adults pointed questions.

Alternative face print is smudged with dirt and has a stunned expression

FIRST IMPRESSIONS
Seamus's first minifigure had freckles and the 2018 Gryffindor torso in Hogwarts Whomping Willow (75953), which added to the expanding castle sets and roster of student minifigures.

2021 Gryffindor torso has a badge on the school jumper

HAVING A BLAST
Poor Seamus has a tendency to attract trouble with magic, from exploding his feather in Charms, to exploding his potion in Snape's class and getting soot all over his minifigure face.

ARGUS FILCH
UNCARING CARETAKER

Unique hair piece includes a bald pate

ARGUS FILCH is a Squib—a non-magical person with magical parents. As caretaker, he keeps the castle in order and the school running smoothly, which includes catching students who are breaking the rules— a task he relishes a little too much.

STUDENTS OUT OF BED!
Filch likes catching students breaking the rules. Though if he had his way, they'd all be punished far more severely than they are!

Bedraggled clothes

Keys because Filch can't open doors with magic

MAGICAL FILE

YEAR: 2018

SET: 75953: Hogwarts Whomping Willow

ACCESSORIES: Lamp

ANIMAL INSTINCT
A scruffier Filch minifigure patrols the castle grounds with his cat, Mrs. Norris. She revels in helping catch naughty students. He's distraught when she is mysteriously petrified.

71

COLIN CREEVEY
ENTHUSIASTIC FIRST-YEAR

Expression of sincere joy and enthusiasm

Hair piece was new for 2021

JOINING HOGWARTS in the year below Harry Potter, Colin Creevey is very excited to make Gryffindor house—just like his hero. Many people are interested in Harry Potter because of his fame, but Colin is truly loyal.

MAGICAL FILE

YEAR: 2021

SET: 76389: Hogwarts Chamber of Secrets

ACCESSORIES: Camera

DID YOU KNOW?

Muggle-born Colin is the first in his family to have any magical ability. His Muggle father is a milkman who knew nothing about magic until Colin got his letter from Hogwarts.

Feet follow Harry around

WHIPPER SNAPPER

Young Colin loves taking photos, and his camera saves his life. He's the first student to be petrified, but if he'd seen the monster without his lens, his fate would have been worse.

JUSTIN FINCH-FLETCHLEY

HUFFLEPUFF STUDENT

AS A MUGGLE-BORN, Justin is at risk when the Chamber of Secrets is opened. Legend says it contains a terrible monster who will purge the school of those considered unworthy to study magic, leaving only pure-blood students unharmed.

Alternative face looks worried about Cornish pixies

MAGICAL FILE

YEAR: 2021
SET: 76389: Hogwarts Chamber of Secrets
ACCESSORIES: Wand, tan-colored owl

Yellow-lined hood is printed on the back of the torso

Cloaked Hufflepuff torso is a unique version of the 2021 house uniform designs

DOUBLE TROUBLE

Professor Lockhart starts a Dueling Club, but it quickly gets out of hand. Harry appears to threaten Justin, who soon after becomes the second student to be petrified.

MISCHIEVOUS MAYHEM

Justin is in class when Professor Lockhart releases blue Cornish pixies. The teacher runs away in panic, leaving the class to fend for themselves as the fiendish creatures create chaos.

73

RON WEASLEY
COURAGEOUS ARACHNOPHOBE

Eyes watch all the spiders while Harry speaks to Aragog

Reverse of head is screaming in terror

CREEPY CRAWLY
This LEGO spider piece, with a central stud connector and eight chunky, arched legs, was first created in 2010.

WHILE HERMIONE IS petrified, Ron and Harry look for clues about events 50 years ago when the Chamber of Secrets first opened. "Follow the spiders," Hagrid said, so they follow the scuttling trail of spiders deep into the Forbidden Forest.

Hands carry a lamp and a broken wand

OFF THE BEATEN TRACK
It would have to be spiders! Of all the creatures Ron could encounter, spiders terrify him the most. Plus, his wand has been misfiring ever since he taped its two halves back together.

MAGICAL FILE

YEAR: 2018
SET: 75950: Aragog's Lair; 75955: Hogwarts Express
ACCESSORIES: Wand, lamp, suitcase, rat

HARRY POTTER

GUTSY INVESTIGATOR

Alternative face is terrified

MAGICAL FILE

YEAR: 2018
SETS: 75950: Aragog's Lair; 75955: Hogwarts Express
ACCESSORIES: Wand, candle

Bones in arm were all removed by Lockhart when he was trying to fix them

WEB OF LIES

Fifty years ago, people thought that baby Aragog was Slytherin's monster and that Hagrid was to blame. He helped Aragog escape to the forest. Now huge, the spider has many children.

Entire minifigure can fit within the grasp of Aragog's legs

DEEP IN THE FORBIDDEN FOREST, Harry asks Aragog, a giant Acromantula, about the events 50 years ago. He says Hagrid is innocent, but he won't tell them about the monster—his kind do not speak its name and they fear it above all others.

DID YOU KNOW?

Harry would be a delicious dinner. Hagrid cared for Aragog and saved his life, so he won't let his children eat Hagrid, but he won't deny them Harry and Ron.

GINNY WEASLEY
PUPPET MASTER'S PREY

Long hair pulled back from face with a clip

Young, freckled face print shared with the first-year Susan Bones minifigure

A GIRL HAS BEEN snatched and taken into the Chamber of Secrets... and it's young Ginny Weasley. As she grows weaker, Voldemort grows stronger and gets closer to returning alive. However, Harry and Ron are on the case.

MAGICAL FILE

YEAR: 2021
SETS: 76389: Hogwarts Chamber of Secrets
ACCESSORIES: Wand, broom

Short legs—Ginny is a first year when she's taken in the Chamber of Secrets

BRIGHT TARGET
Ginny's minifigure is wearing magenta clothes in Diagon Alley (75978) when Lucius Malfoy hides the diary among her school books.

CHARMED AND HARMED
After finding Tom Riddle's diary, Ginny has been using it to communicate with him. Tom can be very persuasive, and he magically manipulates her into opening the Chamber of Secrets for him.

HARRY POTTER

HEIR OF GRYFFINDOR

Eyes are safe from seeing the Basilisk's after Fawkes blinds it with his talons

HARRY CAN HEAR the monster in the Chamber of Secrets because it's a Basilisk—a type of snake. In facing it and Tom Riddle, Harry shows determination and resourcefulness, along with loyalty to Dumbledore and a certain disregard for the rules.

Clothes get drenched and filthy being in the Chamber of Secrets

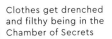

MAGICAL FILE

YEAR: 2021
SETS: 76389: Hogwarts Chamber of Secrets
ACCESSORIES: Wand, Chocolate Frog, Sword of Gryffindor

Hogwarts cloak is unfastened, unlike all the other students' cloaks in this set

FLOO POWDER FACE
This minifigure harks back to the beginning of Harry's year when he shops in Diagon Alley (75978). One face is dirty because of his Floo powder mishap. Whoops!

SERPENT SLAYER
No beast is more deadly than the Basilisk. Instant death awaits anyone who meets its giant serpent eyes. An indirect glance— in a lens, ghost, mirror, or water—causes petrification.

ALBUS DUMBLEDORE
CHAMPION OF MUGGLE-BORNS

Fawkes is a phoenix, just like Dumbledore's Patronus

Pointed hat with a star pattern also appears on Dumbledore's golden anniversary minifigure

RED IN TRIPLICATE
Two other Dumbledore minifigures also wear scarlet robes (with trousers) in Fawkes, Dumbledore's Phoenix (76394) and Hogwarts: Dumbledore's Office (76402).

The first molded LEGO Fawkes piece

AT HOGWARTS, help will always come to those who ask for it. When the Chamber of Secrets is opened, Harry shows such loyalty to Dumbledore that the headmaster's loyal phoenix, Fawkes, swoops to help Harry in his hour of need.

MAGICAL FILE

YEAR: 2020

SET: 71028: LEGO Harry Potter Minifigures Series 2

ACCESSORIES: Fawkes the phoenix, wand

HIGH HOPES
Dumbledore's minifigure has three things to save the day: Fawkes blinds the Basilisk, the Sword of Gryffindor destroys it, and the Sorting Hat delivers the sword to Harry.

TOM RIDDLE
THE HEIR OF SLYTHERIN

LOOK AGAIN at Tom Marvolo Riddle. The letters spell "I am Lord Voldemort." A remnant of the Dark Lord's 16-year-old self has been stored in his diary and Voldemort tries to use it to regain his strength.

Darker version of Cedric Diggory's hair piece

Face shows how Voldemort looked when he was 16 years old

Old-fashioned Hogwarts uniform from 50 years ago

Minifigure is solid, even though Tom Riddle's body is only a stored memory

BOOK WORM
Like Tom himself, his first minifigure came from a book—it was an exclusive with DK's LEGO *Harry Potter: The Magical Treasury*.

MAGICAL FILE

YEAR: 2021

SET: 76389: Hogwarts Chamber of Secrets

ACCESSORIES: Wand, diary

CORRIDOR OF POWER
Behind the snake-covered vault door lies the Chamber of Secrets. Only Voldemort can control its monster, the Basilisk, because he is the Heir of Slytherin.

CHAPTER THREE

HARRY POTTER AND THE PRISONER OF AZKABAN™

A NEW TEACHER WITH SCRATCHES on his face... terrifying Dementors... and rumors of a dangerous escaped prisoner. The Hogwarts Express hasn't even arrived at Hogsmeade yet, but already there are hints that Harry's third year at school will not be straightforward.

Ron Weasley

EXPECTO PATRONUM!

STAN SHUNPIKE

KNIGHT BUS CONDUCTOR

WELCOME TO the Knight Bus—the emergency transportation for stranded witches or wizards. As the conductor, Stan Shunpike wears a bright purple suit to match the bus's striking livery. He greets the passengers, sells tickets, and takes care of the luggage.

MAGICAL FILE

YEAR: 2019
SET: 75957: The Knight Bus
ACCESSORIES: None

Disheveled shirt from too many night shifts

Ticket-printing machine

DID YOU KNOW?

The Knight Bus set contains a whopping 170 purple bricks in 28 designs. The window frame element was made in purple specially for this model.

Purple leg piece is shared with Lavender Brown

MOVER AND SHAKER

Buckle up for a bumpy ride! The triple-decker bus has beds, but they slide around so passengers don't get much sleep. The chandelier also shakes, and the one in this set hangs on a wobbly LEGO® pin.

ERNIE PRANG
KNIGHT BUS DRIVER

Bald patch and white hair are a single LEGO piece

Oversize glasses on a unique head print

NEED A RIDE? Ernie Prang, driver of the bright purple Knight Bus, can take you wherever you want to go. He zips through the streets at high speed, careening around tight corners and squeezing through narrow gaps. Take it away, Ern!

SHRUNKEN MINIFIGURE HEAD
Ernie is accompanied in his cab by a speaking shrunken head. It gives a running commentary on the journey and shouts out obstacles for Ernie to avoid.

Sand-yellow trousers are shared with Remus Lupin

MAGICAL FILE

YEAR: 2019

SET: 75957: The Knight Bus

ACCESSORIES: None

KNIGHT TO THE RESCUE
The Knight Bus appears when a witch or wizard sticks their wand arm in the air. It even works for Harry, who doesn't know the bus exists. It rescues him after he flees the Dursleys.

83

HERMIONE GRANGER
HOGWARTS EXPRESS PASSENGER

Younger hair style is used for some but not all third-year Hermione minifigures

MAGICAL FILE

YEAR: 2018
SET: 75955: Hogwarts Express
ACCESSORIES: Wand, suitcase

LIKE CLOCKWORK
Arriving at King's Cross, Hermione has passed through the Muggle-proof barrier to reach Platform 9¾ in time to catch the Hogwarts Express. It leaves at 11 a.m. every year on September 1st.

Striped hoodie has a new print on the 2022 variant, which looks older than this Hermione

Short leg piece because the set covers events in both the first and third films

HERMIONE IS EXCITED to be headed back to Hogwarts. There are so many new subjects to discover in the third year, such as Divination, Muggle Studies, and Care of Magical Creatures. Where will Hermione find the time to study them all?

CROOKSHANKS
For her third year, Hermione gets a ginger cat called Crookshanks. He accompanies her taller minifigure, which has a more mature hair style and is also from 2018.

REMUS LUPIN
DEFENSE AGAINST THE DARK ARTS PROFESSOR

Scars look like they were made by slashing claws

Face print on the reverse side has large yellow eyes

PROFESSOR LUPIN is the third Defense Against the Dark Arts professor in as many years. He's a compassionate and inspirational teacher with first-hand experience of his subject. Dumbledore welcomes Lupin, even though he knows his terrible secret.

BACK TO SCHOOL
This year on the Hogwarts Express, the new teacher sits among his students. Hermione is very observant. If there were anything unusual about him, she'd be sure to spot it.

Bedraggled clothes suggest Lupin's been having a difficult time

MAGICAL FILE

YEAR: 2018

SET: 75955: Hogwarts Express

ACCESSORIES: Wand, suitcase

MAKE DO AND MEND
Lupin's train-traveling 2022 minifigure wears a darker suit and striped shirt, but times are just as hard. It's in even worse repair, with patches and scratches.

85

DEMENTOR
CHILLING GUARDS OF AZKABAN

Mouth is open, ready to deliver Dementor's Kiss

Eyeless creature finds its way toward victims by sensing emotions

MAGICAL FILE

YEAR: 2018
SET: 75955: Hogwarts Express
ACCESSORIES: None

CHILL IN THE AIR
The Patronus Charm is a force that works as a shield against Dementors. The most advanced ones take the shimmering form of an animal. Harry's is a stag, like his dad's was.

Ribs visible beneath wispy cloak

Twisted, smoke-like transparent base instead of legs

DEMENTORS ARE FOUL creatures who guard the wizard prison, Azkaban, and feed off all positive feelings. A fate worse than death is the Dementor's Kiss, when the creature drains all happiness, leaving victims with only fear and despair.

CHILL IN THE AIR
Harry first encounters Dementors on the Hogwarts Express. They are hunting the escaped convict Sirius Black, but they cause Harry to collapse. Professor Lupin dispatches them.

DRACO MALFOY
CARE OF MAGICAL CREATURES STUDENT

Alternative face is fiercely sneering

DRACO IS MORE THAN

a little arrogant and looks down on Hagrid, so he is not impressed when Hagrid starts teaching Care of Magical Creatures. Hagrid is passionate about animals, but he does tend to underplay the danger they pose.

MONSTER BOOK OF MONSTERS

Hagrid is amused to give Draco and his classmates a book that viciously attacks them. Most don't realize that stroking the book's spine makes it harmless and obedient.

This torso appears on Draco with short legs from when he arrives in Hogwarts: Great Hall (75954)

Medium-size hinged legs for third-year Draco

MAGICAL FILE

YEAR: 2020
SET: 30628: Monster Book of Monsters
ACCESSORIES: Wand

MONSTER-SIZE

Draco comes with a giant-size Monster Book, which has a rolling and snapping play feature. Though the actual textbook has a nasty bite, it is only the size of a regular book.

NEVILLE LONGBOTTOM
CARE OF MAGICAL CREATURES STUDENT

Sleek, side-parting hair piece is also on Neville's waiter minifigure from his sixth year

Perpetual worried expression

NERVOUS NEVILLE worries about many of his classes, but in Care of Magical Creatures there is the possibility of real harm. Not least from his textbook, *The Monster Book of Monsters*—it charges at people and has a vicious bite.

SNAPPING BOOK
Neville's *The Monster Book of Monsters* is hinged with a frilled edge for fur, and has a wedge-shaped tile piece printed with teeth and pages between the covers.

DID YOU KNOW?
Hagrid's third-year students struggle to control their copies of *The Monster Book of Monsters*. Harry had to lure his with a shoe to jump on it and then restrain it with a belt.

Warm cloak because Care of Magical Creatures classes take place outdoors

MAGICAL FILE

YEAR: 2020
SET: 71028: LEGO Harry Potter Minifigures Series 2
ACCESSORIES: *The Monster Book of Monsters*, wand

BOGGART

SHAPESHIFTING FEARMONGER

Professor Snape's face print

SHAPESHIFTING BOGGARTS take the form of their victim's biggest fear—and for Neville Longbottom, that's Professor Snape. To defeat one, you remove the fear by making it look silly, for example, by dressing Snape in Neville's grandmother's clothes.

MAGICAL FILE

YEAR: 2018

SET: 5005254: Harry Potter Minifigure Collection

ACCESSORIES: Red handbag

Neville's grandmother's green suit

Fox stole with a mouse in its mouth

Hand clutches a red handbag

DID YOU KNOW?

Ron's Boggart turns into a giant spidery Acromantula, which he gives eight roller-skates. Harry's is a Dementor, and Professor Lupin's is the full moon because he's a werewolf.

RIDDIKULUS!

In a third-year practical Defense Against the Dark Arts lesson, Professor Lupin lets a Boggart out of a wardrobe so that each student can practice using the Riddikulus charm under pressure.

PERCY WEASLEY

HEAD BOY

All the Weasleys have ginger hair, but only Percy has this curly style

Head Boy badge is worn with great pride

RON'S SELF-IMPORTANT brother Percy Weasley is very ambitious. For now, he is enjoying his status as Head Boy and enforcing the school rules. After Hogwarts, he has his eye on a prestigious job at the Ministry of Magic—the center of political power.

HUMBLE ORIGINS

Percy grows up in The Burrow with his parents, sister, and five brothers. But he is keen to surround himself with people he regards as more impressive than his family.

DID YOU KNOW?

Scabbers the rat used to be Percy's pet. When his parents gave him an owl as a reward for becoming a Hogwarts prefect, Scabbers was passed down to Ron.

Regulation uniform is always neatly worn

MAGICAL FILE

YEAR: 2022

SET: DK's book LEGO *Harry Potter: A Spellbinding Guide to Hogwarts Houses*

ACCESSORIES: Wand

MR. FLUME
CO-OWNER OF HONEYDUKES SWEET SHOP

Lavender hat is unique to this minifigure

Exclusive friendly face print greets customers

Scarf keeps elderly Mr. Flume warm in the wintry weather

AMBROSIUS FLUME runs Honeydukes sweet shop with his wife. They are pillars of the Hogsmeade community, and their homemade delicacies are known far and wide in the wizarding world. They also supply tasty treats for the trolley on the Hogwarts Express.

MAGICAL FILE

YEAR: 2021

SET: 76388: Hogsmeade Village Visit

ACCESSORIES: Acid Pops, Honeydukes box

DID YOU KNOW?
Honeydukes is located in prime position on the main street of Hogsmeade—a purely wizarding village that is completely unknown to Muggles.

WINDOW DRESSING
Honeydukes' large, curved windows tempt in passers-by with their delectable displays of treats and a chocolate fountain. The shop looks particularly inviting with a dusting of snow.

MRS. FLUME

CO-OWNER OF HONEYDUKES SWEET SHOP

Hair scooped up in a loose bun

MRS. FLUME runs Honeydukes sweet shop with her husband. A haven for everything sweet and delicious, their LEGO store is stocked with wizarding treats from Acid Pops, cookies, and popcorn, to lollipops and row upon row of candy jars.

MAGICAL FILE

YEAR: 2021
SET: 76388: Hogsmeade Village Visit
ACCESSORIES: Acid Pops, cookie

Bonbon-inspired print on knitted poncho

Money bag tied around waist

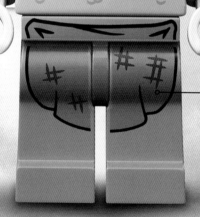

SCHOOL'S OUT!
Hogwarts trips are the icing on the cake for business. When students are allowed on rare visits to Hogsmeade, they flock to Honeydukes to stock up on goodies like Sugar Quills.

ACID POPS
A transparent yellow minifigure head piece with a satin element on top makes a tempting lidded jar of Acid Pops. These sour sweets are a Honeydukes bestseller.

MADAM ROSMERTA
LANDLADY OF THE THREE BROOMSTICKS

Flowing curls in this color are unique to this minifigure

Alternative face print is snarling

Necklace (not made from Butterbeer corks, like Luna's is)

Sleeveless sheepskin jacket

FOR THOSE WANTING a refreshing tankard of Butterbeer poured by a friendly face, look no further than the Three Broomsticks. Madam Rosmerta runs the cozy pub that also serves Gillywater, Firewhisky, elf-made wine, and pumpkin juice.

MAGICAL FILE

YEAR: 2021
SET: 76388: Hogsmeade Village Visit
ACCESSORIES: None

REGULAR CUSTOMER
When Professor McGonagall is in Hogsmeade, she drops by the Three Broomsticks to visit her old friend, Madam Rosmerta, for a frothy Butterbeer and a cozy fireside chat.

WANTED WIZARD!
This term's visit to Hogsmeade takes place under a shadow. Wanted signs warn that the dangerous convict Sirius Black is on the loose. He has broken out of the wizard prison, Azkaban.

MINERVA MCGONAGALL
VISITOR AT THE THREE BROOMSTICKS

Hair is pulled into a tighter bun than Mrs. Flume's hair piece

Alternate face print is frowning sternly

TITTLE TATTLE
The Three Broomsticks is the perfect place to share gossip. It's where an invisible Harry hears that Sirius Black is his godfather and also, incorrectly, that Black betrayed his parents.

MAGICAL FILE

YEAR: 2021
SET: 76388: Hogsmeade Village Visit
ACCESSORIES: Wand, goblet

Back of torso has ornate silver-printed decorations

WHEN PROFESSOR MCGONAGALL visits Hogsmeade with the students during Harry's third year, her minifigure sports a new green robe design. For the first time, her minifigure wears a hair piece instead of a witch's hat.

DID YOU KNOW?
Minerva was the name of the Roman goddess of wisdom. It's the perfect name for wise Minerva McGonagall who prizes knowledge and has dedicated her life to education.

SYBILL TRELAWNEY
DIVINATION PROFESSOR

Wild, frizzy hair is held back with a silk scarf in a single molded piece

Oversize glasses magnify eyes

PROFESSOR TRELAWNEY has made some insightful predictions of life-and-death in her time, but she can't use her inner eye at will, so she often comes across as just eccentric. She teaches Divination and revels in predicting doom and disaster.

FIRST SIGHT
Trelawney's original minifigure from 2018 wore a sloped skirt piece instead of trousered legs, but she still had a teacup for predicting catastrophe—especially for Harry Potter.

Quirky fashion style of layered patterned fabrics and jewelry

MAGICAL FILE

YEAR: 2022

SET: 76396: Hogwarts Moment: Divination Class

ACCESSORIES: Wand, crystal ball, teapot, teacup

A NOBLE ART?
Harry's class studies Divination during the third year. In Trelawney's heavily decorated turret classroom, they try to read the future from the likes of tea leaves, crystal balls, and dreams.

CORNELIUS FUDGE

MINISTER FOR MAGIC

LEGO bowler hat piece dates back to 2012

Clean-shaven face print is shared with Corban Yaxley

FUDGE HAS THE TOP JOB in wizarding politics— Minister for Magic. During his tenure, Draco Malfoy is injured when he provokes Buckbeak the Hippogriff. The innocent animal is sentenced to death by the Ministry, under pressure from Lucius Malfoy.

HATCHET JOB
A sinister masked and hooded executioner accompanies Fudge to carry out the grisly task. He carries the deadly tool of his trade, which has a LEGO ax head that was new for 2019.

Fudge normally wears black suits—not just when overseeing executions

Long, sturdy overcoat for tramping through Hogwarts' muddy grounds

DEATH DUTIES
Fudge arrives at Hagrid's hut to ensure the correct enforcement of Buckbeak's execution. There he is, among the pumpkins, but the next moment, he has disappeared...

MAGICAL FILE

YEAR: 2019

SET: 75947: Hagrid's Hut: Buckbeak's Rescue

ACCESSORIES: None

SIRIUS BLACK
MOST WANTED WIZARD

Beard and hair have grown long and scruffy in prison

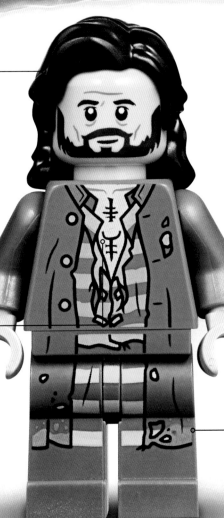

MAGICAL FILE

YEAR: 2019
SET: 75945: Expecto Patronum
ACCESSORIES: None

PRISONERS OF AZKABAN
In 2022, two other disheveled Sirius Black minifigures were on the run; one in the Shrieking Shack and one escaping Hogwarts.

Chest tattoos

Tatty, dirty, Azkaban-issue clothing

HIPPOGRIFF TO THE RESCUE!
After Sirius is recaptured by the Ministry, Harry uses Hermione's Time-Turner to rescue Buckbeak and then break out his godfather. The Hippogriff flies Sirius to a safe hiding place.

EVERYONE FEARS SIRIUS BLACK, who has escaped from Azkaban. But he was imprisoned for a crime he didn't commit, and now he wants to clear his name and see his godson, Harry. Not easy tasks when you're on the run from Dementors!

PETER PETTIGREW

BETRAYER OF FRIENDS

Fur-inspired printing on suit

Facial features have become ratlike after spending so long in his Animagus form

UNCOVERED

In 2022, a variant of Peter Pettigrew, freshly discovered to have been hiding as a rat, appears alongside his betrayed friends in The Shrieking Shack & Whomping Willow (76407).

HIDING IN PLAIN SIGHT

Being a rat for 12 years is not every wizard's cup of pumpkin juice, but it's better than Azkaban. Everyone thought Peter was dead, but he's been living with the Weasleys in his Animagus form.

Hand was willingly sacrificed to the Dark Lord

PETER PETTIGREW was one of the Marauders, along with James Potter, Remus Lupin, and Sirius Black. The best of friends, they always had each other's backs—until Pettigrew ratted them out to Voldemort.

MAGICAL FILE

YEAR: 2019
SET: 75965: The Rise of Voldemort
ACCESSORIES: Wand

REMUS LUPIN
UNFORTUNATE WEREWOLF

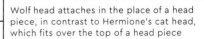

Wolf head attaches in the place of a head piece, in contrast to Hermione's cat head, which fits over the top of a head piece

MAGICAL FILE

YEAR: 2022
SET: 76407: The Shrieking Shack & Whomping Willow
ACCESSORIES: None

TRAGICALLY, PROFESSOR LUPIN was bitten by a werewolf when he was young. Every full moon, he transforms into a wild, beastly werewolf. Each time, he has no memory of his real identity and would attack his best friend if he crossed his path.

BEING HUMAN
A new human Lupin accompanies the wolf, along with a LEGO feature that spins to switch between them. The other side of his face has wolfish yellow eyes and some sprouting stubble.

Molded, bent, doglike leg piece

Tan color matches Lupin's suit in the same set

FAITHFUL FRIENDS
At school, Lupin's friends (James, Sirius, and Peter) took him to the Shrieking Shack every month to keep him safe. The violent Whomping Willow was planted to keep people away.

HARRY POTTER

THIRD-YEAR HERO

Third-year Harry minifigures have a mix of this young hair piece and older styles

DURING HARRY'S eventful third year, he is often seen wearing the same light-blue t-shirt and dark-blue zippered jacket. In this outfit, Harry rides the Knight Bus, time travels, and saves Buckbeak, Sirius Black, and even himself.

MAGICAL FILE

YEAR: 2019
SETS: 75957: The Knight Bus; 75947: Hagrid's Hut: Buckbeak's Rescue; 75945: Expecto Patronum
ACCESSORIES: Trunk, newspaper, wand

Zippered-jacket torso is also worn by an older Harry with full-size legs in 12 Grimmauld Place (76408)

Medium-size leg piece for third-year Harry

BOYS IN BLUE
Variants of Harry's minifigure sneak into Hogsmeade Village Visit (76388) and appear with a muddy t-shirt in the Shrieking Shack (76407) and Hogwarts Hospital Wing (76398).

STAG SHIELD
Professor Lupin teaches Harry how to draw on a powerful happy memory to conjure a Patronus as protection against Dementors. His takes the form of a stag—just like his dad's.

RON WEASLEY

INJURED HERO

> Young hair piece is used for some third-year Ron minifigures

THE SIGHT of the dreaded Grim—a fierce black dog and omen of death—terrifies Ron, but it gets worse when the creature bites his leg and drags him into a tunnel under the Whomping Willow. The dog turns out to be Sirius Black's Animagus form.

A RISK WITH EVERY MOUTHFUL

One of Ron's visitors brings him a box of Bertie Bott's Every Flavor Beans. They really do mean *every* flavor. Some are delicious, but you could get the taste of vomit or earwax.

> Clothes are ripped from being dragged by Sirius's Animagus

> White plaster cast

MAGICAL FILE

YEAR: 2022

SETS: 76398: Hogwarts Hospital Wing

ACCESSORIES: Walking stick

OUT ON A LIMB

Sirius Black didn't mean Ron any harm—he was after Scabbers, aka Peter Pettigrew. But that does not make Ron's injury any less real, nor his stay in the hospital wing any shorter.

POPPY POMFREY
SCHOOL HOSPITAL MATRON

Unique nurse-style headpiece

THE WIZARDING WORLD has healers instead of doctors. Madam Pomfrey is an expert healer and she looks after everyone's health and well-being at Hogwarts. She is kept super busy with all kinds of magical maladies and mishaps.

MAGICAL FILE

YEAR: 2022
SET: 76398: Hogwarts Hospital Wing
ACCESSORIES: Clipboard with medical chart

Upside-down watch face is easily read by minifigure

Wide, elasticated belt with metal clasp

HEALING HANDS
During Harry's second year, Madam Pomfrey has to regrow all of the bones in his arm after Professor Lockhart botches a fracture repair and makes them all disappear.

Clean, white medical robes

BONE-FIDE RESULTS
One of Madam Pomfrey's remedies is Skele-Gro. It can fix or rebuild witches' and wizards' bones, but this takes all night and is a very painful procedure.

HERMIONE GRANGER
TIME TRAVELER

Alternate face is gripped with pain

Third-year hairstyle has no bangs

GOOD TIMING
In Hogwarts Hospital Wing, Hermione's minifigure has a handheld LEGO Time-Turner. She and Harry retrace their steps to save two innocent creatures: Buckbeak and Sirius.

HOW CAN SOMEBODY be in two places at once? With a Time-Turner! Hermione has been using this magical gadget to travel in time so that she can take extra classes. However, this magic can be unpredictable and only allows someone to go back a few hours.

Removable cast because arm is injured by the Whomping Willow

Jacket is zipped up higher than on the first minifigure variant

MAGICAL FILE

YEAR: 2022

SET: 76407: The Shrieking Shack & Whomping Willow; 76398: Hogwarts Hospital Wing

ACCESSORIES: Wand, Time-Turner, arm cast

FIRST TIME AROUND
An earlier variant of this Hermione minifigure from 2019 wears the same outfit, but has a printed Time-Turner hanging around her neck.

CHAPTER FOUR

HARRY POTTER AND THE GOBLET OF FIRE™

TO EVERYONE'S GREAT EXCITEMENT, Harry's fourth year brings the thrilling Triwizard Tournament to Hogwarts. But for Harry, who unexpectedly finds himself caught up in the competition, it holds grueling challenges and unprecedented dangers.

Hungarian Horntail

I DIDN'T PUT MY NAME IN THE CUP! I DON'T WANT ETERNAL GLORY!
Harry Potter—Triwizard Champion
Hungarian Horntail

HARRY POTTER

FOURTH-YEAR

Lightning scar on Harry's head is painful again

This longer hair piece with sideswept bangs is only used for fourth year Harry minifigures

NOW BEGINNING HIS fourth year at Hogwarts, Harry has grown. Both his LEGO® legs and hair are longer. In an ominous development, his scar has begun to hurt. The last time that happened, it meant that Voldemort was nearby.

MAGICAL FILE

YEAR: 2022
SET: 76396: Hogwarts Moment: Divination Class
ACCESSORIES: Teacup, wand

2021 Gryffindor torso appears on both short- and long-legged minifigures

THE INNER EYE

Harry doesn't know it, but Professor Trelawney made a prophecy which has had a profound effect on his life. It caused Voldemort to go after him and his parents 14 years ago.

OWL POST

Hedwig is very useful for carrying messages from Harry to his godfather, Sirius Black. Sirius is in hiding from the Ministry of Magic because of a crime he didn't commit.

ALBUS DUMBLEDORE
HOST OF THE TRIWIZARD TOURNAMENT

Flat hat mold was seen in blue on Dumbledore's 2018 minifigure

Beard piece gathered with a tie is new for 2019

IN HARRY'S FOURTH YEAR, Hogwarts is honored with hosting the Triwizard Tournament. The legendary event brings together three schools for a series of magical contests. As headmaster, Dumbledore declares the competition open.

CHOCOLATE FROG CARDS
Tasty chocolate frogs come with collectible cards of celebrated witches and wizards, and Dumbledore, of course. In 2022, LEGO versions were inserted into sets at random.

Faded, lavender robes are worn during Harry's fourth year

MAGICAL FILE

YEAR: 2019

SET: 75948: Hogwarts Clock Tower

ACCESSORIES: None

TWINKLETOES
Part of the Triwizard Tournament is the dazzling Yule Ball. The Triwizard champions open the dancing, then Dumbledore takes to the floor along with other teachers and students.

107

MAD-EYE MOODY
DEFENSE AGAINST THE DARK ARTS PROFESSOR

Head and hair can be swapped for separate Barty Crouch, Jr., pieces

Spinning magical eye is very powerful

GRUFF ALASTOR

"Mad-Eye" Moody may be an alarming sight, but he's a celebrated Auror—a dark-wizard catcher. Half the cells in Azkaban are full thanks to him. Now he's the new Defense Against the Dark Arts professor, but all is not as it seems.

MAGICAL FILE

YEAR: 2022
SET: 76397: Hogwarts Moment: Defence Against the Dark Arts
ACCESSORIES: Staff, flask of Polyjuice Potion, textbook

Prosthetic leg due to battling Dark wizards

MASTER OF DISGUISE
Mad-Eye Moody's first minifigure, from 2018, hints at his real identity. Turning the head around reveals a face print that looks like Barty Crouch, Jr.

SUBSTITUTE TEACHER
The new teacher's strange, unstable behavior is a clue to his real identity: Barty Crouch, Jr., is a Death Eater and uses Polyjuice Potion to pose as Mad-Eye Moody to get close to Harry.

NEVILLE LONGBOTTOM
TROUBLED STUDENT

Hair piece in this color is also used for Ron's minifigure when he turns into Gregory Goyle with Polyjuice Potion

Alternative face print looks very distressed

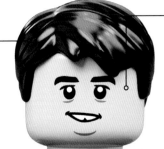

DARK SPELLS
The Cruciatus Curse and Avada Kedavra are two of the three Unforgivable curses. Use these spells and you'll get a one-way ticket to Azkaban.

CRUEL CLASS
Mad-Eye Moody (who is Barty Crouch, Jr., in disguise) takes a practical approach to teaching. He demonstrates the three Unforgivable Curses on an enlarged spider.

This Gryffindor torso, with an open cloak, is also worn by Harry, Ron, and Hermione

MAGICAL FILE

YEAR: 2022
SET: 76397: Hogwarts Moment: Defence Against the Dark Arts Class
ACCESSORIES: Wand, magnifying glass

MANY STUDENTS STRUGGLE with Defense Against the Dark Arts, but Neville finds a demonstration of three illegal curses particularly traumatic because he has personal experience of them: his parents were destroyed by the Cruciatus Curse.

FLEUR DELACOUR
VISITOR FROM BEAUXBATONS

Elegant, felt school hat piece has built-in hair

MAGICAL FILE

YEAR: 2019
SET: 75958: Beauxbatons' Carriage: Arrival at Hogwarts
ACCESSORIES: Teacup, letter

TALENTED FLEUR DELACOUR is a fine example of the best Beauxbatons Academy of Magic has to offer. The girls from the French school are all accompanied by their headmistress, Madame Maxime, and are the first to arrive at Hogwarts.

Short, collared cape covers top of arms

Dual-printed legs for silk skirt and tights

LITTLE SISTER
Gabrielle Delacour accompanies her older sister to Hogwarts. She wears the same uniform, but has a younger face print and shorter legs than Fleur.

WELCOME WAGON
The Beauxbatons students travel by air in an ornate carriage drawn by all-white Abraxan winged horses. The carriage itself is delicate and elegant, but it lurches precariously.

FLEUR DELACOUR

BEAUXBATONS CHAMPION

Alternate face print looks terrified

MAGICAL FILE

YEAR: 2019
SET: 75946: Hungarian Horntail Triwizard Challenge
ACCESSORIES: Wand, goblet

THE FIRST TASK
The four contestants in the Triwizard Tournament have a Champions' tent for rest and refreshments. They draw straws to see who gets which dragon. Fleur draws and outwits the Welsh Green.

Quilted clothing to protect from dragon claws

Back of torso is printed with a large "B" logo for Beauxbatons

A GOOD EGG
As well as being each contestant's ticket to the following round, the egg contains a clue about what faces them next. This LEGO golden egg was created especially for this set.

BRAVE AND DETERMINED Fleur Delacour is selected by the Goblet of Fire to be the Triwizard Champion for Beauxbatons school. In the first task, each contender must face a dragon and retrieve an egg from its nest unscathed.

VIKTOR KRUM

DURMSTRANG CHAMPION

Alternate face print is frowning

WORLD-FAMOUS QUIDDITCH

Seeker Viktor Krum plays for Bulgaria—and he caught the Golden Snitch in the World Cup final. Yet the celebrity sportsman is still at school! He attends the notorious Durmstrang Institute and is selected as their Triwizard Champion.

MAKING WAVES

The students from Durmstrang travel under water, emerging majestically from the lake next to Hogwarts. A mini model of their magnificent sailing ship came in the 2020 Advent Calendar.

Double-headed eagle and stag's head are the symbol of Durmstrang Institute

MAGICAL FILE

YEAR: 2019
SET: 75946: Hungarian Horntail Triwizard Challenge
ACCESSORIES: Wand

INTENT ON TRIUMPH

In the Champions' tent, Krum considers how to conjure a charm to blind and confuse the Chinese Fireball dragon that's his obstacle to the egg and eternal glory.

CEDRIC DIGGORY
HOGWARTS TRIWIZARD CHAMPION

17-YEAR-OLD CEDRIC FROM Hufflepuff house was selected by the Goblet of Fire to be the Hogwarts Champion in the Triwizard Tournament. Once chosen, there's no going back. He expects to be the only one—until the goblet also produces Harry's name.

Alternate face is fiercely scowling

Hufflepuff-colored robes despite Cedric representing his whole school

Back of torso reads "DIGGORY," though the middle of the word is obscured by his hood

FINAL TASK
In 2018, Cedric's minifigure wears his Hufflepuff outfit from the third task. Cedric reaches the Triwizard Cup—but it brings him face to face with Voldemort.

MAGICAL FILE

YEAR: 2019

SET: 75946: Hungarian Horntail Triwizard Challenge

ACCESSORIES: Wand

IN THE LINE OF FIRE
Scorching breath, saber-sharp claws, and thrashing tails await the Champions in the first task as each faces a dragon. However Cedric survives his encounter with the Swedish Short-Snout.

HARRY POTTER
UNEXPECTED TRIWIZARD CHAMPION

HARRY'S NAME mysteriously finds its way into the Goblet of Fire—and is selected for the Triwizard Tournament. He doesn't want to compete, but the Goblet forms a binding magical contract. For the first time in the game's history, one school has two contestants.

New-style brick-built broom with a handcuff piece for foot supports

MAGICAL FILE

YEAR: 2022
SET: 76406: Hungarian Horntail Dragon
ACCESSORIES: Wand, broom

"POTTER" is printed on the back of torso

Dual-molded arms are also printed with yellow stripes and stars

HUNGARIAN HORNTAIL

Harry faces the most vicious of the four dragons. He plays to his strengths, summoning his broom and using his Quidditch skills to dodge the beast and grab the golden egg.

Shortest legs of the four Triwizard Champions

TRIWIZARD TRIO

Two other Harry minifigures wear red-and-black competition robes. In 2019, one faces a LEGO Hungarian Horntail, and the other witnesses the Rise of Voldemort.

RITA SKEETER
DAILY PROPHET JOURNALIST

Inquisitive eyes peer over printed glasses

Quick-Quotes Quill can write by itself while Rita asks the questions

BEWARE REPORTER
Rita Skeeter and her Quick-Quotes Quill! Her pen isn't sharp enough to be a physical weapon, but it's good at destroying reputations and spreading false information. Rita's sharp words are influential—but not always true.

MAGICAL FILE

YEAR: 2023
SET: DK's LEGO Harry Potter: *Character Encyclopedia*
ACCESSORIES: Green Quick-Quotes Quill

Sharp tailoring in lime green is part of her creative, individual style

GLEEFUL GOSSIPMONGER
With her eye on the next juicy scoop, Rita relishes the chance to tell the story of the brave and glamorous Triwizard Champions. But she never lets the truth get in the way of a good story.

DID YOU KNOW?
Rita Skeeter's only minifigure was produced specially for this book. It's the third exclusive LEGO Harry Potter minifigure for DK, following Tom Riddle and Percy Weasley.

FRED WEASLEY
GEORGE'S PARTNER IN MISCHEIF

INVENTIVE AND CREATIVE, Fred and his twin brother George always have a scheme going. Eagle-eyed at spotting money-making opportunities, they use the Triwizard Tournament to make some Galleons by taking bets on the outcome.

Open mouth is calling out the odds

Hair has grown longer during the twins' sixth year

MAGICAL FILE

YEAR: 2020

SET: 71028: LEGO Harry Potter Minifigures Series 2

ACCESSORIES: Bookmaker's briefcase

Torso matches George's except that the jacket is buttoned up

BOOKIE'S BAG
Fred's briefcase contains a chalkboard marked up with the odds for the four Triwizard contestants, along with two 1×1 colorful, numbered tiles for bets.

TRIWIZARD CUP
Why should the winner of the Triwizard Cup be the only one to get cash and glory? Fred and George tempt people to be winners themselves by betting on who will lift the trophy.

GEORGE WEASLEY
FRED'S PARTNER IN MISCHIEF

Matching woolly hats worn by both Weasley twins

Alternate face print has closed, laughing eyes

GEORGE AND FRED
solemnly swear that they are up to no good. Ron Weasley's troublemaking twin brothers always have something up their matching sleeves. Their escapades are legendary, and have often been helped by the Marauder's Map.

MARAUDER'S MAP
Invented by James Potter and his friends, the Marauders, this magical map reveals the location of everyone in Hogwarts. Having made good use of it, Fred and George gift it to Harry.

Dual-molded legs

MAGICAL FILE

YEAR: 2020

SET: 71028: LEGO Harry Potter Minifigures Series 2

ACCESSORIES: The Marauder's Map

GOBLET OF FIRE
Fred and George try to submit their names to the Goblet of Fire to compete even though they're under 17. Their Aging Potion doesn't work and the boys sprout long beards.

FLEUR DELACOUR
BEAUXBATONS VIP

This ponytail style is also worn by Fleur for battling the dragon in the first task

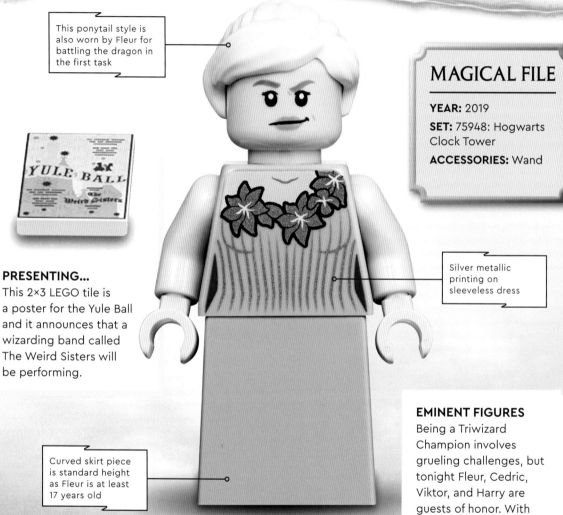

MAGICAL FILE

YEAR: 2019
SET: 75948: Hogwarts Clock Tower
ACCESSORIES: Wand

Silver metallic printing on sleeveless dress

PRESENTING...
This 2×3 LEGO tile is a poster for the Yule Ball and it announces that a wizarding band called The Weird Sisters will be performing.

Curved skirt piece is standard height as Fleur is at least 17 years old

EMINENT FIGURES
Being a Triwizard Champion involves grueling challenges, but tonight Fleur, Cedric, Viktor, and Harry are guests of honor. With their dance partners, they open the ball.

AT THE GRAND YULE BALL, Fleur dazzles in a shimmery, silvery dress. The Triwizard Tournament is about international friendships and magical cooperation, so it's a Triwizard tradition that on Christmas Eve night, everyone gathers for festive frivolity.

VIKTOR KRUM

DURMSTRANG VIP

Same face printing as Krum's minifigure in the first task

ALL EYES ARE ON heartthrob Viktor Krum—the "Bulgarian Bonbon"—to see who he has invited to the ball. The dashing celebrity arrives in his traditional scarlet Durmstrang dress uniform with... Hermione Granger on his arm.

Fur stole printing continues on back

Metallic-printed belt buckle decorated with Durmstrang stag

MAGICAL FILE

YEAR: 2019

SET: 75948: Hogwarts Clock Tower

ACCESSORIES: Wand

TURNING HEADS
First and foremost, the Yule Ball is a dance. Hogwarts Clock Tower (75948) includes a revolving LEGO dancefloor with spots for four couples to spin the night away.

119

HERMIONE GRANGER
VIKTOR'S YULE BALL PARTNER

CHRISTMAS STAR
As well as attending the Yule Ball, Hermione's minifigure brings some festive magic to the LEGO Harry Potter Advent Calendar set in 2020.

MAGICAL FILE

YEAR: 2019
SETS: 75948: Hogwarts Clock Tower; 75981: Harry Potter Advent Calendar (2020)
ACCESSORIES: Wand

Silver-printed details

Different colored bricks create an ombré effect of blended shades of fabric

Three-quarter height skirt built with a 1×2 LEGO brick and 1×2 plate

BACK TO CLASS
In her fourth year, Hermione's Gryffindor minifigure stands taller than younger ones. She has medium-size legs and a more mature hair style, with no bangs and less frizz.

HERMIONE IS WELL known for her stunning spells, but at the Yule Ball, she stuns everyone with her appearance. She makes an entrance looking beautiful, with sleek, glossy hair and an exquisite dress with elegant ripples of floaty pink fabric.

CEDRIC DIGGORY
HUFFLEPUFF VIP

CHOSEN BY THE GOBLET OF FIRE

At the Yule Ball in Hogwarts Clock Tower (75948), the Goblet of Fire stands by the entrance as a reminder of the Triwizard Tournament. Its blue flame stands on a golden goblet.

THE PRIDE OF HUFFLEPUFF, Cedric Diggory cuts a dashing figure in his elegant black wizarding dress robes. Kind, honest, and brave Cedric is also exceptionally hardworking, fair-minded, and a fierce friend.

Back of torso has a pointy printed hood rather than a suit collar

Cedric wears a black bow tie in contrast to Harry's white one

Black legs are longer than Harry's

MAGICAL FILE

YEAR: 2019

SET: 75948: Hogwarts Clock Tower

ACCESSORIES: Wand

DID YOU KNOW?

Cedric is a keen Quidditch player and he plays on the Hufflepuff team as Seeker— the same position as Harry Potter. All-around talented, he is also a Hogwarts Prefect.

CHO CHANG
CEDRIC'S YULE BALL PARTNER

Alternative face print is sad

MAGICAL FILE

YEAR: 2020
SET: 75981: Harry Potter Advent Calendar (2020)
ACCESSORIES: Wand

FOR THE RECORD
Students prepare for the ball with dance lessons, accompanied by a magical gramophone. Though on the night, they dance along to a live orchestra and the band, The Weird Sisters.

Chinese-inspired cheongsam-style silk dress

Fifth-year's skirt is shorter than a regular sloped skirt piece

A HOGWARTS STUDENT of Chinese heritage, Cho Chang is in Ravenclaw house in the year above Harry. He asks her to go to the Yule Ball, but he's too late—she's already accepted an invitation from the other Hogwarts Triwizard Champion, Cedric Diggory.

SHORT AND SWEET
A younger Cho Chang in Ravenclaw colors studies alongside Harry and Professor Flitwick in Hogwarts Moment: Charms Class (76385).

HARRY POTTER

GRYFFINDOR VIP

Alternate face printing looks happy

Modern wizarding dress robes

WITH PLENTY OF GALLEONS in his vault at Gringotts Bank, Harry can splash out on some fashionable dress robes for the ball so his minifigure looks very dapper. He wears a crisp dress shirt, white bow tie, and black waistcoat under his robes.

CHRISTMAS CHEER

The LEGO Harry Potter Advent Calendar sets count down to Christmas with far more festive merriment and excitement than Harry ever experienced at the Dursleys' house.

MAGICAL FILE

YEAR: 2019
SET: 75948: Hogwarts Clock Tower; 75981: Harry Potter Advent Calendar (2020)
ACCESSORIES: Book

Medium-size articulated legs make Harry shorter than the other Champions

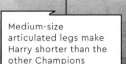

A NEW BROOM

The 2020 Advent Calendar set includes a Firebolt broomstick, wrapped in brown paper. Harry receives it from a mysterious benefactor.

PARVATI PATIL

HARRY'S YULE BALL PARTNER

FRED AND GEORGE aren't the only minifigure twins at Hogwarts. Parvati and Padma are identical sisters in Harry's year. The sisters attend the Yule Ball in coordinating formal dress inspired by their Indian heritage.

A few strands of hair are elegantly gathered together at the back

SILENT PARTNERS
Parvati is excited to accompany Harry, a Triwizard Champion, to the ball, but her evening does not go well. Ron and Harry are terrible company and all but ignore them.

Embroidered details are printed in metallic silver

Indian style of dress is a chaniya-choli or ghagra-choli

PROUD GRYFFINDOR
Parvati's second minifigure reads about the Grim—a black dog and a terrible omen—in her favorite lesson in Hogwarts Moment: Divination Class (76396).

MAGICAL FILE

YEAR: 2020
SET: 75981: Harry Potter Advent Calendar (2020)
ACCESSORIES: Wand

PADMA PATIL

RON'S YULE BALL PARTNER

Hair and head pieces are shared by the identical twins

MAGICAL FILE

YEAR: 2020

SET: 75981: Harry Potter Advent Calendar (2020)

ACCESSORIES: Wand

The dupata is a scarf of thin, light fabric that wraps across the torso

The lower part of the outfit is a skirt called a chaniya

MAKING THE BEST OF IT

Other guests like Cho Chang are much better company than Ron. He is uncomfortable and miserable and refuses to dance with Padma.

POOR PADMA goes to the Yule Ball with a very grumpy Ron. Her blouse, or choli, is the same bright pink as her sister's main outfit, and her chaniya and dupatta are the same salmon pink as Parvati's choli. Their outfits have matching decorations.

DID YOU KNOW?

In the fifth year, Padma and Parvati both join Harry's group called Dumbledore's Army. He teaches them how to protect themselves against Voldemort and his Death Eaters.

RON WEASLEY
PADMA'S YULE BALL PARTNER

Alternative face print is glum to match his mood at the Yule Ball

PARTY POOPER

Ron hated learning to dance and he plans to sit down as much as possible this evening, however enchanting the music is.

Frilly lace collar is very unfashionable

Embarrassing second-hand robes

MERLIN'S BEARD! What is Ron wearing? These are traditional dress robes sent by his mother, but they're so outdated that Ron feels like his Great Aunt Tessie. Although one side of his minifigure's face is smiling, Ron spends the Yule Ball being miserable.

MAGICAL FILE

YEAR: 2019

SET: 75948: Hogwarts Clock Tower; 75981: Harry Potter Advent Calendar (2020)

ACCESSORIES: Wand

RUBEUS HAGRID

DRESSED-UP GROUNDSKEEPER

MAGICAL FILE

YEAR: 2019

SET: 75958:
Beauxbatons' Carriage:
Arrival at Hogwarts

ACCESSORIES: Two
traffic paddles,
teacup

Hair-and-beard piece
is unique to
Hagrid's
minifigures

EVEN SCRUFFY HAGRID makes an effort to dress up for the Yule Ball. Under his shaggy brown dress robes, he has a fresh white shirt and a bright, polka-dot tie. The glittering, festive ball is a far cry from the muddy grounds of Hogwarts.

HORSE WHISPERER

Hagrid sees the good in all creatures and enjoys caring for them. He looks after the Abraxan winged horses, including feeding them the finest produce. They are very particular.

This is the second LEGO print for this custom-molded large minifigure piece

Regular-size arm pieces attach to oversize body

INTERNATIONAL RELATIONS

Kind, gentle Hagrid is a good friend of Harry, Ron, and Hermione's, but in Harry's fourth year, he forms a new, special friendship with Olympe Maxime, from Beauxbatons.

OLYMPE MAXIME

BEAUXBATONS HEADMISTRESS

Alternative face looks very sad, like she's about to cry

HEADMISTRESS of Beauxbatons, Olympe Maxime accompanies her young ladies to Hogwarts. As a half-giant, she is the tallest Harry Potter minifigure. She finds a kindred spirit in fellow half-giant Hagrid, and the sweet pair hit it off.

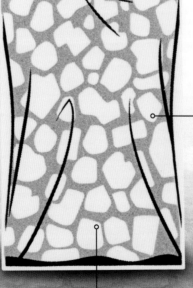

HIGH TEA
Equally tall and patterned, Madame Maxime's first minifigure is dressed in a striking fur-collared winter coat in Beauxbatons' Carriage: Arrival at Hogwarts (75958).

Fabric pattern is printed on the back of the torso and skirt

CORDIAL RELATIONS
As the representatives of their schools, Madame Maxime and Dumbledore lead the Yule Ball celebrations to further magical cooperation between their countries.

Skirt is a sloped piece three LEGO bricks high

MAGICAL FILE

YEAR: 2019

SET: 75948: Hogwarts Clock Tower

ACCESSORIES: None

FILIUS FLITWICK
CHOIR MASTER

Mouth is open wide in song

MAGICAL FILE

YEAR: 2019
SET: 75964: Harry Potter Advent Calendar (2019)
ACCESSORIES: Wand

FLITWICK'S MINIFIGURE'S short stature and bushy eyebrows are about all he has in common with his first minifigure, but he is still the same cheery Charms teacher. This is how Professor Flitwick looks from Harry's third year onward.

Jacket removed so Flitwick can move his arms more easily when conducting

Detachable bow-tie piece

MUSICAL MASTER
Filius Flitwick's extensive skills stretch beyond Charms and dueling—to music. He conducts the orchestra and organizes the music for the Yule Ball.

LOUD AND CLEAR
The part-goblin Head of Ravenclaw house has a similar style minifigure from 2018. He carries a megaphone to be heard at the Yule Ball.

VIKTOR KRUM
SHARK-HEADED SWIMMER

FOR THE SECOND TASK, each Triwizard Champion must find a way to breathe underwater in order to retrieve something important from the bottom of the Black Lake. Viktor Krum's solution is to partially transfigure himself into a shark.

Shark head fits over a regular minifigure head piece with a large mouth print

Reverse head print is Viktor's regular face

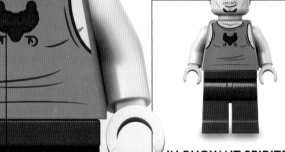

Durmstrang emblem features on every Viktor Krum minifigure

IN BUOYANT SPIRITS
With his shark head swapped for a regular head and hair piece, Viktor has a confident smile, a stubbly moustache, and goatee beard.

HIDDEN TREASURE
Champions must rescue what they hold most dear: Hermione for Viktor, and Ron for Harry. Their minifigures, in a magical sleep, float in the lake, supported by flexible LEGO elements.

MAGICAL FILE

YEAR: 2023
SET: 76420: Triwizard Tournament: The Black Lake
ACCESSORIES: Wand

HARRY POTTER

GILLED SWIMMER

Gills for breathing underwater are printed on face

Wand for fending off attacks from vicious Grindylows

MAGICAL FILE

YEAR: 2023

SET: 76420: Triwizard Tournament: The Black Lake

ACCESSORIES: Wand, cup, flippers

HARRY VENTURES INTO the deep, murky waters of the Black Lake with Gillyweed—a magical plant that gives him gills and webbed hands and feet. His new elongated body powers through the water and allows him to breathe for up to an hour.

TRUE HERO
Harry returns to the pier after the time limit. Showing true mettle and compassion, he wouldn't leave any of the merpeople's prisoners until he knew they were being rescued.

MERPEOPLE OF THE LAKE
One sand-green minifigure with water-swept golden hair stands guard over the enchanted "guests." Ron and Hermione will be released only to their rightful Triwizard Champion.

LEGO flippers in Harry's skin color are his feet that have lengthened and grown webbed toes

LORD VOLDEMORT
THE DARK LORD RETURNED

AT THE GRAVE OF HIS FATHER, Tom Riddle, Sr., Voldemort sees his plan come together. Peter Pettigrew resurrects the Dark Lord with a nasty potion. Having been transported to the graveyard by Voldemort, Harry unwittingly helps with his revival.

Single face print because minifigure has no hair or hat

Grave expression is replaced with a jeering face and sticking-out tongue for the 2022 Advent Calendar variant of this minifigure

Body isn't fully human, but it's powerful and very much alive

MAGICAL FILE

YEAR: 2019
SET: 75965: The Rise of Voldemort
ACCESSORIES: Wand

DIMINISHED BUT NOT DEFEATED

For 14 years, Voldemort was reduced to a weak, mewling creature. This LEGO mold was first created in 2016 for a baby wrapped in a papoose.

RISEN FROM THE GRAVE

The grave over which Harry and Voldemort duel, has a LEGO hinge. The ground flips up and thrusts Lord Voldemort's new minifigure up from the earth.

DEATH EATER
FOLLOWER OF VOLDEMORT

New LEGO hat piece for 2019 is unique to this set

Creepy metallic mask hides each person's true identity

THE DARK LORD has risen and his Death Eater supporters flock to his side in the Little Hangleton graveyard. They come because of their loyalty and support for their master—or perhaps they're just too afraid not to show up.

GRAVE PERIL
Harry Potter is in the Death Eaters' grasp, but they're not allowed to attack him. Voldemort wants Harry for himself, but he's underestimated the young wizard's power.

DEATHLY HALLOWS
This grave could belong to Ignotus Peverell from Godric's Hollow because it has the sign of the Deathly Hallows. Legend has it that these three magical objects can conquer death.

MAGICAL FILE

YEAR: 2019

SET: 75965: The Rise of Voldemort

ACCESSORIES: Wand

Long black robes match the Dark Lord's

CHAPTER FIVE

HARRY POTTER AND THE ORDER OF THE PHOENIX™

THE HEADQUARTERS OF THE ORDER OF THE PHOENIX MAY BE FOUND AT NUMBER TWELVE, GRIMMAULD PLACE, LONDON.

Kingsley Shacklebolt

Harry Potter

Fred and George Weasley

SIRIUS BLACK
HARRY'S GODFATHER

Angry scowl at being confined to 12 Grimmauld Place

MAGICAL FILE

YEAR: 2022
SET: 76408: 12 Grimmauld Place
ACCESSORIES: Wand

SIRIUS IS STILL IN HIDING

from the Ministry, but 12 Grimmauld Place has some home comforts. He shares his family house with the Order of the Phoenix—a secret society created to fight Voldemort— but he's frustrated he can't get out there and do more.

Neat, clean clothes since getting rid of his grimy prison garb

Dapper pinstripe velvet jacket in olive green is printed on both torso and legs

THE NOBLE HOUSE OF BLACK

Sirius comes from an ancient wizarding line whose family tree decorates the wallpaper. But, as he explains to Harry, his relatives were pure-blood supremacists who erased him from it.

PADFOOT

As an Animagus, Sirius can disguise himself as a shaggy black dog whenever he likes, as seen in The Shrieking Shack & Whomping Willow (76407).

NYMPHADORA TONKS
AUROR

Purple hair piece also features on Tonks's minifigure in the 2022 Advent Calendar (76404)

Alternative face print has an entertaining pig's snout

"TONKS," AS NYMPHADORA prefers to be called, is a loyal member of the Order of the Phoenix. After Hogwarts, she joined the Ministry of Magic where she trained as an Auror, and her dark-wizard-hunting skills are very valuable to the Order indeed.

FEELING LOW
Although she's normally cheerful and bubbly, when Tonks is unhappy, she struggles to change her appearance. Her hair turns mousy brown, as in Attack on the Burrow (75980).

Gray flying-gloves

MAGICAL FILE

YEAR: 2022

SET: 76408: 12 Grimmauld Place

ACCESSORIES: Comet 260 broom, wand

SHAPESHIFTER
At the dinner table, Tonks entertains everyone by using her rare, genetic Metamorphmagus ability. She can change her appearance into anything she wants—like her face into a pig's.

KINGSLEY SHACKLEBOLT
SENIOR AUROR

Nigerian-style cap

A POWERFUL AUROR
Kingsley Shacklebolt works for the Ministry while secretly serving the Order of the Phoenix. This means he can hinder the Ministry's efforts to find Sirius Black and also feed useful information to the Order.

BOLT FROM THE BLUE
Shacklebolt's first minifigure, from 2018, wears a printed cap and a detachable fabric piece for the outer layer of his colorful robes.

RESCUE PARTY
As a member of the Order, Shacklebolt is a regular visitor to 12 Grimmauld Place. He's also one of the group who delivers Harry there during the summer before Harry's fifth year.

Printed stole rather than the fabric one worn by his first minifigure

Wizard robes were inspired by traditional Nigerian styles, including a ceremonial robe called an agbada

MAGICAL FILE

YEAR: 2022
SET: 76408: 12 Grimmauld Place
ACCESSORIES: Wand, broom

RON WEASLEY
FIFTH-YEAR GRYFFINDOR

This longer, sideswept hair piece is used from Ron's fifth year onward

Alternative face print is frowning

Unique T-shirt torso piece

DID YOU KNOW?

12 Grimmauld Place is a terraced London townhouse magically concealed between two Muggle homes. Unplottable on a map and protected by a Fidelius Charm, it's perfect as the headquarters for the Order of the Phoenix.

MAGICAL FILE

YEAR: 2022
SET: 76408: 12 Grimmauld Place
ACCESSORIES: Wand

DIRTY WORK
While Ron helps Molly clean the dark, gloomy house, the *Daily Prophet* is busy tarnishing Harry and Dumbledore's names in order to discredit the rumors that Voldemort's back.

RON SPENDS THE SUMMER holiday at 12 Grimmauld Place. He longs to join the Order of the Phoenix, but he's too young and his mother won't stand for it. He has to make do with Fred and George's Extendable Ears to listen in on the Order's secrets.

KREACHER
CORRUPTED HOUSE-ELF

Mouth constantly mutters insults and complaints

Hard headpiece is nonflexible plastic, unlike Dobby's head

Eyes narrowed in hate for Harry Potter

HOME MAKER
These two LEGO® houses slide apart to reveal the Blacks' home—12 Grimmauld Place. Kreacher was its proud house-elf until Sirius arrived and filled it with "undesirables."

GRUESOME BELONGINGS
The Blacks had an unhealthy interest in the Dark Arts and they collected dangerous and grisly objects like this minifigure skull in a dome. Kreacher loyally looks after it all.

KREACHER WAS FANATICALLY KEEN on the cruel Black family. He served them loyally, but he does not like Sirius. The unpleasant house-elf does as little for his new master as his magical bindings will allow—while muttering under his breath.

MAGICAL FILE

YEAR: 2022

SET: 76408: 12 Grimmauld Place

ACCESSORIES: Black umbrella

DOLORES UMBRIDGE

MEDDLER FROM THE MINISTRY

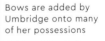

Bows are added by Umbridge onto many of her possessions

MAGICAL FILE

YEAR: 2020

SET: 75967: Forbidden Forest: Umbridge's Encounter

ACCESSORIES: Wand

Cats, especially kittens, are a favorite decoration

DON'T BE FOOLED

by Umbridge's soft pink outfits and sugary smile. She is not soft and not sweet. She's a cruel and scheming witch who arrives from the Ministry of Magic to teach Defense Against the Dark Arts, but she has bigger plans.

IN THE PINK

All Umbridge's minifigures wear pink from head to toe and cat motifs as brooches or even a stole. The first carries a cup of Veritaserum —truth potion—for forcing student confessions.

Pink high-heeled shoes

SUPER-SIZE SAVER

Hagrid's brutish half-brother Grawp is a full giant and he comes to Harry and Hermione's aid when they lure Umbridge into the Forbidden Forest.

HARRY POTTER

DEFENDER AGAINST THE DARK ARTS

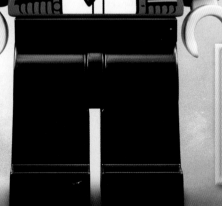

HARRY KNOWS THAT
Voldemort has returned, but the Ministry denies it and is interfering with the teaching at Hogwarts. Harry and his friends take matters into their own hands. If they're not being taught to defend themselves, Harry will teach them instead!

Harry has cut his hair shorter for the fifth year

This face print is used for Harry's minifigures from the third year onward

Unfastened Gryffindor cardigan is worn only by this minifigure

FIFTH-YEAR FASHIONS
Minifigure variants of Harry in his fifth year uniform also feature Gryffindor torsos with a gray V-neck sweater and black robes fastened up.

MAGICAL FILE

YEAR: 2022
SET: 75966: Hogwarts Room of Requirement
ACCESSORIES: Wand

GLOWING SUCCESS
Conjuring a corporeal Patronus is a very advanced protective spell. Under Harry's expert guidance, many of his friends learn to do it.

HERMIONE GRANGER

FOUNDER OF DUMBLEDORE'S ARMY

Brown version of Padma and Parvati Patil and Cho Chang's black hair piece

Expression reveals that Hermione finds it slightly thrilling to be breaking the school rules

MAGICAL FILE

YEAR: 2020
SET: 75966: Hogwarts Room of Requirement
ACCESSORIES: Wand

RESOURCEFUL HERMIONE

believes that students can learn from Harry's experience of battling the Dark Arts. It's thanks to her that their group gets off the ground. They call it Dumbledore's Army (DA)—even though Dumbledore knows nothing about it.

MAGICAL SHIELD

Clever Hermione is one of the first to produce a successful Patronus charm. Hers is an otter, and its transparent-blue LEGO piece captures the magical guardian's shimmering form.

Buttoned-up Hogwarts cardigan worn only by this Hermione minifigure

THE COME-AND-GO ROOM

The DA needs a secret place to meet, and the magical Room of Requirement comes to their aid. It appears only when someone needs it—it's almost as if Hogwarts wants them to fight back!

DEATH EATER DUMMY
TARGET PRACTICE

Minifigure hood piece was first created in 2008

Face printing is based on a Death Eater's mask

THE ROOM OF REQUIREMENT provides whatever is needed, including a wooden mannequin for students to practice their defensive spells on. The magic of the room knows just what the DA is up against, so it cleverly re-creates the look of a real Death Eater.

DA DISPLAY
The Room also conjured up a noticeboard for important DA business, including inspirational photos of Cedric and the original Order of the Phoenix who fought Voldemort 15 years ago.

MAGICAL FILE

YEAR: 2020

SET: 75966: Hogwarts Room of Requirement

ACCESSORIES: None

Ideal target zone

Wheels instead of feet so figure is easy to move around

BEST PRACTICE
The mannequin on wheels can take no end of spells, like *Expelliarmus!* for disarming and *Stupefy!* for stunning. It can even prompt Patronus Charms for defeating Dementors.

HANNAH ABBOTT

HUFFLEPUFF MEMBER OF DUMBLEDORE'S ARMY

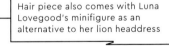

Hair piece also comes with Luna Lovegood's minifigure as an alternative to her lion headdress

MAGICAL FILE

YEAR: 2020
SET: 40419: Hogwarts Students Accessory Set
ACCESSORIES: Wand, lamp

HANNAH ABBOTT IS A fifth-year Hufflepuff who signs up to Dumbledore's Army. Even though she's a Prefect, Hannah believes it's right to break Professor Umbridge's strict school rules to fight against her cruel, unfair regime, and learn defensive magic.

SAFE HAVEN

In 2023, Hannah's second minifigure wears yellow-edged black robes. A sociable Hufflepuff, she lets her hair down in the house common room with Cedric Diggory and Susan Bones.

Yellow-and-black torso is first worn in 2018 by fellow Hufflepuff, Susan Bones

SLIDING WALLS

As a DA member, Hannah is taught by Harry in the Room of Requirement. The LEGO model has a sliding wall panel outside the door because the secret room is usually concealed.

LUNA LOVEGOOD
RAVENCLAW MEMBER OF DUMBLEDORE'S ARMY

NEVER ONE TO FOLLOW
the crowd, Luna Lovegood doesn't hesitate to join Dumbledore's Army. Some of her quirky beliefs could be down to the eccentric *Quibbler* newspaper she reads—which she's even been known to look at upside-down.

MAGICAL FILE

YEAR: 2022
SET: 76400: Hogwarts Carriage and Thestrals
ACCESSORIES: Shoulder bag, Thestral food, wand, *Quibbler*

Thestral food

Medium-size leg piece because Luna is in the year below Harry

Shoulder bag holds meat for feeding Thestrals

Bare feet—mean students keep hiding Luna's shoes

BEWARE NARGLES!
Only Luna wears a Butterbeer-cork necklace. She believes it fends off mysterious creatures called Nargles. Perhaps her younger minifigure also has one under her robes.

PAIR OF LONERS
Like Harry in his fifth year, Luna can see the gentle but eerie Thestrals who pull the Hogwarts carriages. To anyone who hasn't seen death, the black, winged creatures are invisible.

CHO CHANG

RAVENCLAW MEMBER OF DUMBLEDORE'S ARMY

Wavier hair piece than on previous Cho minifigures

Alternative expression is upset about Cedric

CHO CHANG SIGNS UP for Dumbledore's Army. She was very close to Cedric and feels his loss so she understands the need to learn protective spells. Perhaps she's also interested in joining because the teacher is a certain Harry Potter.

CHRISTMAS TRYST

At the last DA meeting of term, Cho and Harry share a special moment together under a sprig of mistletoe. It's provided by the always considerate Room of Requirement.

Full-size minifigure legs because Cho is in the sixth year

MAGICAL FILE

YEAR: 2020

SET: 40419: Hogwarts Students Accessory Set

ACCESSORIES: Wand, book

TWO FOR JOY

In 2018, Cho had the first LEGO Ravenclaw torso along with a removable fabric skirt. Her 2021 version has the same hair style but a new face print and shorter legs.

147

MICHAEL CORNER
POPULAR RAVENCLAW

Hair piece shared with Sirius Black

MAGICAL FILE

YEAR: 2023
SET: 76411: Ravenclaw™ House Banner, 2023
ACCESSORIES: Wand

THE FIRST MALE MINIFIGURE

to wear a Ravenclaw uniform, Michael Corner started Hogwarts at the same time as Harry. In the fifth year, he believes the rumors that Voldemort is back, and he signs up to Dumbledore's Army.

First Ravenclaw torso to have a cardigan

Michael can produce a noncorporeal Patronus with his wand

DID YOU KNOW?

During his time at Hogwarts, Michael has close relationships with Ginny Weasley and Cho Chang.

COMMON VALUES

Michael's House, Ravenclaw, prizes knowledge and intelligence above all. To enter the house common room, people aren't required to give a password but to answer a riddle.

CENTAUR

PURE-BRED SPECIES THAT'S PART-HUMAN, PART HORSE

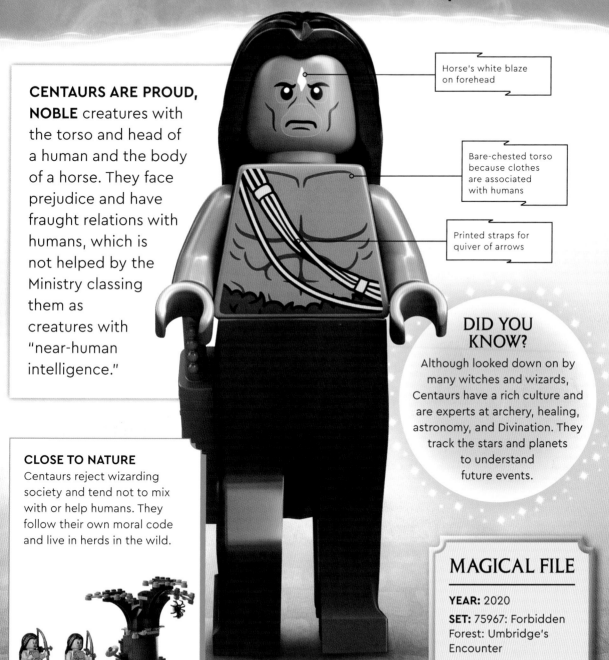

CENTAURS ARE PROUD, NOBLE creatures with the torso and head of a human and the body of a horse. They face prejudice and have fraught relations with humans, which is not helped by the Ministry classing them as creatures with "near-human intelligence."

Horse's white blaze on forehead

Bare-chested torso because clothes are associated with humans

Printed straps for quiver of arrows

DID YOU KNOW?

Although looked down on by many witches and wizards, Centaurs have a rich culture and are experts at archery, healing, astronomy, and Divination. They track the stars and planets to understand future events.

CLOSE TO NATURE

Centaurs reject wizarding society and tend not to mix with or help humans. They follow their own moral code and live in herds in the wild.

MAGICAL FILE

YEAR: 2020

SET: 75967: Forbidden Forest: Umbridge's Encounter

ACCESSORIES: Bow and arrow, quiver

HERMIONE GRANGER
GRAWP'S FAVORITE

MAGICAL FILE

YEAR: 2020

SET: 75967: Forbidden Forest: Umbridge's Encounter

ACCESSORIES: Wand, bicycle bell

Alternative face print looks fierce and angry

Freckles appear on Hermione's face print from third year onward

Striped Muggle sweater has three House colors on gray, but no Slytherin green

NOT-SO-GENTLE GIANT

Grawp means well, but he doesn't know his own strength. As a token of his affection, he gives Hermione some bicycle handlebars with a bell and tries to communicate with her by ringing it.

DID YOU KNOW?

When Hagrid discovers he has a half-brother, he wants to help him, even though Grawp's a wild giant. Hagrid brings him to the Forbidden Forest. After all, they are the only family each of them has.

QUICK-THINKING HERMIONE throws Umbridge off the scent when the DA is exposed. She leads her into the Forbidden Forest, where fierce creatures dwell. One, who doesn't mean any harm but is still dangerous, is Hagrid's giant half-brother, Grawp.

HARRY POTTER
OUT OF UNIFORM

Harry's minifigures use this shorter hair piece from the fifth year onward

Turn the head piece around to see Harry frowning

MAGICAL FILE

YEAR: 2020
SETS: 75967: Forbidden Forest: Umbridge's Encounter; 75980: Attack on the Burrow
ACCESSORIES: Wand

ALL GROWN UP
Arriving at 12 Grimmauld Place (76408), Harry wears a torso from two of his third year minifigures with a blue zipped jacket, but now his legs are longer and his hair is shorter.

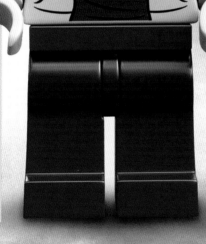

Hand is injured in detentions with cruel Professor Umbridge

A GIANT REQUEST
Hagrid asks Harry and Hermione to look after his giant half-brother, Grawp. The huge wild creature can feed himself, but Hagrid wants him to have some friendly company.

WHEN NOT IN LESSONS, Harry likes to wear casual clothes. In this outfit, his minifigure ventures into the Forbidden Forest and visits The Burrow during the Christmas holidays. However, the festivities are abruptly halted when Death Eaters attack.

CHAPTER SIX

HARRY POTTER AND THE HALF-BLOOD PRINCE™

I DIDN'T MAKE THE CUT FOR THE SLUG CLUB. IT'S OKAY.

MY WON-WON!

Ron Weasley and Lavender Brown

HARRY'S SIXTH YEAR brings fun and frivolity but also serious study. Harry enjoys success in Quidditch and in the Potions classroom, and Dumbledore lets him in on crucial knowledge about Voldemort. But sinister forces are gaining in strength and even Hogwarts itself is under threat.

TO HOGWARTS' BEST AND BRIGHTEST!

Professor Slughorn

Luna Lovegood

Harry Potter

Neville Longbottom

Hermione Granger

ALBUS DUMBLEDORE
HARRY'S MENTOR

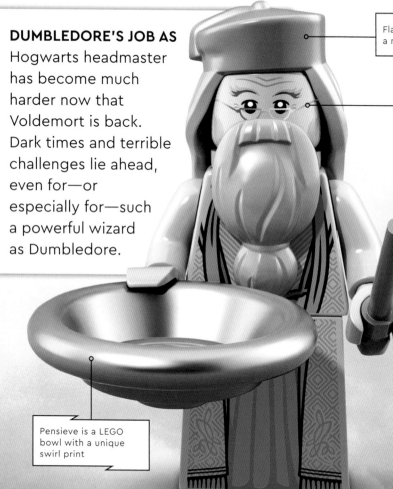

DUMBLEDORE'S JOB AS
Hogwarts headmaster
has become much
harder now that
Voldemort is back.
Dark times and terrible
challenges lie ahead,
even for—or
especially for—such
a powerful wizard
as Dumbledore.

Flat hat with a tassel is
a new piece in 2018

Dumbledore's silver,
rather than gold,
half-moon spectacles first
appear on this minifigure

Pensieve is a LEGO
bowl with a unique
swirl print

MAGICAL FILE

YEAR: 2018

SET: 71022 LEGO®
Harry Potter Minifigures
Series 1

ACCESSORIES:
Pensieve, wand

SWORD OF GRYFFINDOR
Dumbledore keeps the
Sword of Gryffindor in
his office. Imbued with a
powerful substance, it can
destroy Horcruxes—Dark
magical objects that contain
pieces of Voldemort's soul.

BLAST FROM THE PAST
Memory like a sieve? Store
them in a Pensieve so you
can revisit them any time!
Dumbledore shares
memories of Tom Riddle
with Harry, giving him
crucial information for
defeating him.

HORACE SLUGHORN
SLYTHERIN POTIONS MASTER

Hair and head pieces are common to both Slughorn's minifigures

JOVIAL BUT VAIN, Horace Slughorn surrounds himself with the most talented, famous, and powerful witches and wizards, whom he collects like trophies. The Potions Master comes out of retirement to resume his post in Harry's sixth year.

WELL-CONNECTED
Professor Slughorn's portly frame was first stuffed into tweed robes for a minifigure in 2018. His everyday four-piece suit has detailed printing, including a chain for his pocket watch.

Tassels decorate tweed and velvet dress robes

Waistcoat for parties has more elaborate decoration than Horace's everyday ones

MAGICAL FILE

YEAR: 2020

SET: 75969: Hogwarts Astronomy Tower

ACCESSORIES: Potions book, wine glass, scissors

IN THE CHAIR
Slughorn is on the run from Death Eaters so when a visitor arrives, he disguises himself as a plump armchair with plenty of stuffing. But this doesn't fool Dumbledore, who reveals his head.

FRED WEASLEY

CO-CREATOR OF WEASLEYS' WIZARD WHEEZES

Expression on reverse side of head is grinning

MAGICAL FILE

YEAR: 2020
SET: 75978: Diagon Alley
ACCESSORIES: None

FRED AND GEORGE LOVE making mischief and now they've found a way to make money from it. Galleons are pouring into their new joke shop, Weasleys' Wizard Wheezes. The twins have become smart, young businessmen about town.

"W" logo for the shop

Formality of three-piece business suit counterbalanced with quirky bright stripes

MAGICAL MAYHEM
Everything about Weasleys' Wizard Wheezes grabs attention, including its technicolor building. A hinged arm lifts the hat of the large figure sprouting from the window.

OFF DUTY
Fred and George Weasley never stop pranking, but when they're relaxing in 12 Grimmauld Place (76408), they wear less formal—but still matching —trousers and shirts.

GEORGE WEASLEY
CO-CREATOR OF WEASLEYS' WIZARD WHEEZES

The twins like to sport identical hair styles

Alternative face print is roaring with laughter

HAVING ESCAPED BORING old school, George and Fred are thriving. Their creations demonstrate their remarkable magical skills, entrepreneurial streak, and mischievous sense of fun. In these dark times, people need a laugh more than ever.

DOUBLE ACT
Fred and George's 2022 minifigures are identical except for their head pieces—which each character shares with its two other minifigures.

The brothers' ties flash

MAGICAL FILE

YEAR: 2020

SET: 75978: Diagon Alley

ACCESSORIES: None

SHENANIGANS FOR ALL
The joke shop is jam-packed with magical delights like fake wands and love potions. Their Skiving Snackboxes contain Fainting Fancies, Nosebleed Nougat, and Puking Pastilles.

LUNA LOVEGOOD
QUIRKY RAVENCLAW

AN INDEPENDENT THINKER, Luna embraces her own fashion style along with many unusual views. She claims that Spectrespecs enable you to see Wrackspurts. Apparently they're creatures that float in your ears and make your brain fuzzy.

Colorful Spectrespecs are a free giveaway with the *Quibbler* newspaper

HOT OFF THE PRESS
Luna carries a printed tile of the tabloid newspaper that her eccentric father edits. Most witches and wizards think the *Quibbler* is nothing but a load of nonsense.

Fabric skirt is replaced with a matching print for the 2022 minifigure variant

Bright blue tights are part of Luna's independent style

BRAVE AT HEART
Although a Ravenclaw, Luna cheers on her friends' Gryffindor Quidditch team when they play Slytherin—even to the point of wearing an elaborate lion headdress!

MAGICAL FILE

YEAR: 2018

SET: 71022: LEGO Harry Potter Minifigures Series 1

ACCESSORIES: *Quibbler* newspaper, shoulder bag

HARRY POTTER
DUMBLEDORE'S AGENT

FOR THE FIRST Hogsmeade visit of his sixth year, Harry and his friends wear their own clothes and head to the Three Broomsticks for a glass of Butterbeer. Harry may look like he's just relaxing, but he's on a mission from Dumbledore.

Alternative expression is an exclusive print of Harry looking alarmed

MAGICAL FILE

YEAR: 2020
SET: 71028: LEGO Harry Potter Minifigures Series 2
ACCESSORIES: *Advanced Potion-Making* book with a tile about the Sectumsempra spell, wand

Seams of jeans printed on side of legs

Gray zippered jacket also worn on Harry's very similar 2022 minifigure, along with a white t-shirt and jeans

ULTERIOR MOTIVE
While Harry, Ron, and Hermione sip Butterbeer, Harry tries to befriend Horace Slughorn—or let himself be "collected" by the vain professor. It's on Dumbledore's orders.

DID YOU KNOW?
Professor Slughorn holds a secret that is crucial to Dumbledore's plan to defeat Voldemort. Harry must find a way to get Slughorn to share this memory—not an easy task as it's not flattering to the old Potions Master.

159

HERMIONE GRANGER
THREE BROOMSTICKS CUSTOMER

Printed Butterbeer accessory is new for Hermione and Ron minifigures in 2020

Printed cowl neck on sweater

DUMBLEDORE'S ARMY

Hermione Granger
Ron Weasley
Harry Potter
George Weasley
Fred Weasley
Ginny Weasley
Luna Lovegood
Neville Longbottom

ON THE RECORD
During another Hogsmeade visit, Hermione helped found Dumbledore's Army. This list she created was signed by the recruits and it features in Hogwarts Students Accessory Set (40419).

DID YOU KNOW?
There have been two series of Collectible Minifigures in the LEGO Harry Potter range, in 2018 and 2020. They each contain 16 minifigures with accessories from across all the films.

Dual-molded legs for jeans, turned-over socks, and snow boots

HERMIONE AND RON from the Three Broomsticks appear with Harry in the second series of Collectible Minifigures, each with a glass of frothy Butterbeer. The figures celebrate the trio's snowy trip to Hogsmeade in their sixth year.

MAGICAL FILE

YEAR: 2020

SET: 71028: LEGO Harry Potter Minifigures Series 2

ACCESSORIES: Butterbeer, wand

RON WEASLEY
LAVENDER'S BOYFRIEND

Alternative face print looks fed up

Long, sideswept hair is a new style for Ron in 2020, used for his fifth-year onward

MAGICAL FILE

YEAR: 2020
SET: 75969: Hogwarts Astronomy Tower
ACCESSORIES: Goblet

WHEN RON INCORRECTLY believes that Harry slipped him some Felix Felicis (luck potion), he has a great day. He plays brilliantly in goal against the Slytherin Quidditch team, he is hailed as a hero by his team, and he gets a girlfriend—Lavender Brown.

Unique torso shows the turquoise patterned shirt Ron is wearing when Lavender first kisses him

DOUBLE DANGER
During his sixth year, Ron wears casual clothes in the Three Broomsticks and at home for Christmas. Both events end in attacks from Dark witches and wizards.

FIRST LOVE
Ron might not impress Professor Slughorn or get invited to his parties, but Lavender couldn't be more obsessed if she'd taken the love potion, Amortentia. She thinks he's fantastic.

LAVENDER BROWN

RON'S GIRLFRIEND

Hair piece has a tiny hole at the back for attaching a pink bow

LOVE IS IN THE AIR in the Gryffindor common room this year. Passionate Lavender Brown falls for Ron Weasley and is completely besotted. The pair become a couple, but their relationship runs its course before the end of the school year.

MAGICAL FILE

YEAR: 2020
SET: 75969: Hogwarts Astronomy Tower
ACCESSORIES: Goblet

Heart prints on torso match Lavender's romantic outlook

DID YOU KNOW?

Lavender wears a long chain with two pendants hanging from it. For Christmas, she also gives Ron a gaudy, sentimental gold necklace that makes him cringe.

Purple trouser piece shared with Stan Shunpike, conductor of the Knight Bus

TRAIN OF THOUGHT

When traveling home for Christmas on the Hogwarts Express, Lavender has only one thing on her mind: her "Won-Won." She draws their initials around a heart on the window pane.

HARRY POTTER
SLUGHORN'S FAVORITE

Head print was first introduced in 2019 for third-year sets

Dark-red shirt and tie worn to the Slug Club Christmas party

HARRY IS EVERYTHING
Professor Slughorn values—talented, famous, powerful. The prospect of teaching him tempts Slughorn back to Hogwarts, and he invites Harry into his exclusive "Slug Club" of students he thinks are destined for greatness.

FELIX FELICIS
Harry earns a vial of Felix Felicis—commonly known as "liquid luck"—from Professor Slughorn for brewing the best Draught of Living Death in Potions class.

Long black dress robes for formal occasions

MAGICAL FILE

YEAR: 2020
SET: 75969: Hogwarts Astronomy Tower
ACCESSORIES: Wand

STROKE OF LUCK
Luck is on Harry's side when he needs to find Slughorn. He runs into the Potions Master in the Herbology greenhouse, sneakily taking clippings of Tentacula plants.

LUNA LOVEGOOD

HARRY'S PLUS ONE

DREAMY LUNA doesn't grab Slughorn's attention as someone with great potential, so she isn't invited into his inner circle. But she does attend his "Slug Club" Christmas party as Harry's guest. Luna isn't used to having friends and going to parties.

Five Luna minifigures have this long blonde hair piece

MAGICAL FILE

YEAR: 2020
SET: 75969: Hogwarts Astronomy Tower
ACCESSORIES: Potion bottle

Frilly layers of party dress fan out like a Christmas tree

Dual-molded legs with black tights and shoes

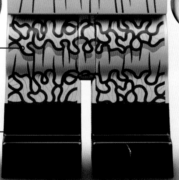

DEFENSIVE CHARM
Each Patronus charm animal is unique to the wizard or witch who conjures it. Luna's is a hare, which she learns to produce in DA lessons with Harry's guidance.

BEDTIME READING
Halfway up the Hogwarts Astronomy Tower (75969), Luna reads a classic edition of the *Daily Prophet* in the blue-themed Ravenclaw dormitory.

HERMIONE GRANGER

SLUG CLUB MEMBER

Hair piece first used for a Hermione minifigure in the Room of Requirement

Alternative face print is angry—perhaps at the Half-Blood Prince

CLEVER HERMIONE is always ready with the right answer in class, and her intelligence catches Professor Slughorn's eye. He invites her to join his exclusive "Slug Club," which includes supper clubs and a Christmas party.

DID YOU KNOW?

In her first lesson with Slughorn, Hermione correctly identifies four potions: Veritaserum (truth-telling serum), Polyjuice Potion (for impersonating someone), Amortentia (love potion), and Felix Felicis ("liquid luck").

Pink cocktail dress worn to sixth-year Christmas party

MAGICAL FILE

YEAR: 2020

SET: 75969: Hogwarts Astronomy Tower

ACCESSORIES: Wand

PARTIES AND POTIONS
Hogwarts Astronomy Tower (75969) also features a Potions lesson. Harry steals Hermione's thunder, but he's using a book with notes by the mysterious Half-Blood Prince. That's cheating!

GINNY WEASLEY

DINNER GUEST

GINNY, THE YOUNGEST

Weasley, is now a fifth-year and her minifigures look much older. Her bold spirit and magical skill impress Professor Slughorn so he invites her to a supper for select students. On the menu are big servings of profiteroles.

Ginny curled her usually straight hair for Slughorn's dinner

Large dessert of profiteroles served to each guest

Shiny green party dress worn to first supper club of the school year

MAGICAL FILE

YEAR: 2020

SET: 71028: LEGO Harry Potter Minifigures Series 2

ACCESSORIES: Dessert of profiteroles

SWEET TREATS

As a member of the "Slug Club," Ginny also attends Slughorn's Christmas party, where the mead flows, along with a chocolate fountain. But it's best to avoid the dragon ball canapés.

HOME FOR CHRISTMAS

After the yule party, Ginny goes home to The Burrow for the holidays. As Ginny is now in the fifth year, both these minifigures have full-size hinged leg pieces.

NEVILLE LONGBOTTOM

SLUG CLUB WAITER

Smoother hair piece with side part is shared with Neville's 2020 minifigure which carries *The Monster Book of Monsters*

DID YOU KNOW?

Since Neville was a baby, his parents have been permanent patients at St. Mungo's Hospital for Magical Maladies and Injuries because of Voldemort. His formidable grandmother, Augusta Longbottom, has raised him. She is strict, but ultimately he makes her proud.

MAGICAL FILE

YEAR: 2020

SET: 75969: Hogwarts Astronomy Tower

ACCESSORIES: Tray and glass, bottle

Formal waiter's uniform with white gloves

WIZARD SERVICE

Slughorn is short-sighted in missing Neville's skill and potential, but Neville doesn't mind waiting on his friends. It could be worse— he could be handing out towels in the bathroom.

SOME STUDENTS are invited to Professor Slughorn's parties, while others serve them drinks. The professor was briefly interested in Neville because his parents bravely fought Voldemort, but he soon snubs the shy, awkward boy and makes him serve drinks.

BLAISE ZABINI

ARROGANT SLYTHERIN

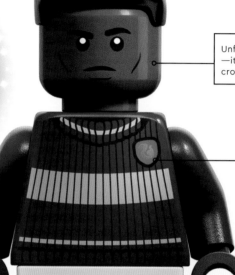

DID YOU KNOW?

Blaise is scathing when Draco tries to show off about his connections to the Dark Lord. Although he shares some views with Voldemort, Blaise is contemptuous of those who follow him.

Unfriendly expression —it's best not to cross Blaise

Quidditch ribbed sweater—Blaise plays as Chaser for Slytherin

New Quidditch wear design released in 2023

MAGICAL FILE

YEAR: 2023
SET: 76410: Slytherin™ House Banner
ACCESSORIES: Wand, broom

COOL CROWD

Vain and haughty, Blaise oozes "cool" in Slytherin, where many (but not all) aspire to be like him. He rules the roost in the grand, dungeon-like common room with disdain and cool detachment.

PRIVILEGED AND WELL-CONNECTED, Blaise Zabini is unimpressed by pretty much everyone—even Draco Malfoy. He shares his view on pure-blood superiority with Salazar Slytherin and assumes he'll have a place in the invite-only Slug Club—and he's right.

DRACO MALFOY

NEW RECRUIT FOR THE DEATH EATERS

DRACO GOES INTO his sixth year with a terrible burden. Now that his father's in Azkaban for being a Death Eater, it falls to him to do Voldemort's bidding. The Dark Lord is angry and punishes the Malfoys by giving Draco a seemingly impossible task.

Sixth-year Draco minifigures have this side-parting hair piece rather than his younger swept-back style

Neutral expression on other side of face

BAD APPLE

Draco uses an apple to test the Vanishing Cabinets he's repairing. In 2022, his minifigure arrives at school in what looks like a Death Eater suit with an added splash of Slytherin.

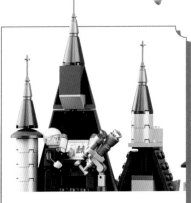

TALL ORDER

Against the odds, Draco finds a way to smuggle Death Eaters into the castle. He fixes a pair of Vanishing Cabinets so they can form a passageway between Borgin and Burkes and the school.

Full-size articulated legs

MAGICAL FILE

YEAR: 2020

SET: 75969: Hogwarts Astronomy Tower

ACCESSORIES: Broom, wand

MOLLY WEASLEY
MATRIARCH OF THE BURROW

All three of Molly's minifigures wear her trademark hair piece

MAGICAL FILE

YEAR: 2020
SET: 75980: Attack on the Burrow
ACCESSORIES: Wand, teapot, broom

MOLLY WEASLEY IS ALWAYS busy at The Burrow. In her cozy home, she raises her seven children and welcomes many others, including Harry. There are often extra visitors for dinner, like old friend Remus Lupin and the Auror Tonks.

Hand-knitted cardigan decorated with mismatching crocheted flowers

Cardigan tied together with twists of yarn

SECOND HOME
At 12 Grimmauld Place (76408), Molly's minifigure is in new chintzy prints. She works hard fixing up the old house and creating a refuge for her family and the Order of the Phoenix.

CLOCK WATCHING
Pride of place in the kitchen is Molly's magical clock. Instead of the time, it gives the location of everyone in the family. It could be "home," "work," "traveling," and hopefully not "mortal peril."

ARTHUR WEASLEY

RON'S DAD

AS WELL AS being father to Ginny, Ron, Fred, George, Percy, Charlie, and Bill, Arthur Weasley works for the Ministry of Magic. He is also a member of the Order of the Phoenix, the secret society fighting Voldemort, which is incredibly dangerous work.

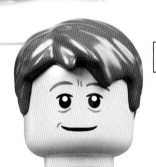

Striped woolen tie

MAGICAL FILE

YEAR: 2020
SET: 75980: Attack on the Burrow
ACCESSORIES: Wand, teacup

Knitted squares sewn together to make a woolen patchwork cardigan

Even at home, Arthur often wears a shirt and tie but in brighter colors than for work

COLLECTIBLE CLUTTER

In his Ministry office, Arthur gets to indulge his obsession with Muggle objects like airplanes, a rubber duck, and a radio. He tinkers with them, fascinated to understand how they work.

SUITED AND BOOTED

As head of the Office for the Detection and Confiscation of Counterfeit Defensive Spells and Protective Objects, Arthur wears a three-piece, gray pinstripe suit.

BELLATRIX LESTRANGE
VOLDEMORT'S MOST DEVOUT DISCIPLE

Elaborate asymmetrical hair piece is unique to Bellatrix's two minifigures

PRISON WEAR
In prison, Bellatrix rails against her chains—and LEGO handcuffs. But she doesn't serve her time—she escapes Azkaban in a mass breakout of Dark witches and wizards.

Corset made of leather pieces stitched together

DRACO MALFOY'S AUNT
Bellatrix Lestrange supports and follows Voldemort with fervid passion, and she longs to be the most devoted and highly praised of all his followers. She is a dangerous witch who enjoys being cruel.

Ornate silver embroidery on dress

MAGICAL FILE

YEAR: 2020

SET: 75980: Attack on the Burrow

ACCESSORIES: Wand

BLEAK MIDWINTER
Forget the season of good will. At Christmas, Bellatrix has a merry time attacking the Weasley family at The Burrow, where she arrives in a plume of dark smoke.

FENRIR GREYBACK

BARBAROUS WEREWOLF

Permanent hair on forehead

Wolfish grin with sharp, pointy teeth

Scars from previous battles

FENRIR IS ANYTHING but ordinary... he is a werewolf. Werewolf witches and wizards are normally only affected during the full moon, but Greyback is wolfish all month long. He loves being a werewolf and relishes all the power it brings him.

MAGICAL FILE

YEAR: 2020
SET: 75980: Attack on the Burrow
ACCESSORIES: Wand

HOT PURSUIT
Like an animal hunting its prey, Fenrir uses his heightened tracking senses when he and Bellatrix chase Harry and Ginny in the cornfields outside The Burrow.

DID YOU KNOW?
The word "lycanthropy" refers to being a werewolf. Witches and wizards turn into a werewolf if they are bitten by one who is transformed during a full moon.

173

CHAPTER SEVEN

HARRY POTTER AND THE DEATHLY HALLOWS™

MAFALDA HOPKIRK
ASSISTANT IN THE IMPROPER USE OF MAGIC OFFICE

Nervous expression because infiltrating the Ministry is high risk and very dangerous

Sharp tailored jacket with wide lapels

BECAUSE MAFALDA HOPKIRK works at the Ministry of Magic, she gets drawn into Harry, Ron, and Hermione's plan to sneak into the offices. They're after Umbridge's locket—one of seven objects they must destroy to defeat Voldemort.

POTION FOR DISGUISE
Hermione brews Polyjuice Potion (featured in set 76391 with Wormwood Infusion, Asphodel, and Gillyweed). She uses it to transform into Mafalda.

Mishmash of printed fabrics—flowery blouse with striped jacket

RUN!
Turning Mafalda's head piece around reveals Hermione's face. The set also comes with Hermione's hair piece for completing her look when the potion wears off.

MAGICAL FILE

YEAR: 2022
SET: 76403: The Ministry of Magic
ACCESSORIES: Black briefcase, wand

REGINALD CATTERMOLE
MAGICAL MAINTENANCE DEPARTMENT WORKER

Water marks from the rain in Yaxley's office

MAGICAL FILE

YEAR: 2022
SET: 76403: The Ministry of Magic
ACCESSORIES: Wand

RON PICKS A BAD DAY
to transform into Reg Cattermole to sneak into the Ministry. He gets in fine, but Reg's Muggle-born wife is on trial, and Reg needs to fix the rain problem in Yaxley's office—his wife's fate could depend on it.

Woolen waistcoat isn't as fancy as the suits of more senior officials

Thin gray overcoat marks him out as working for the Magical Maintenance department

CAUGHT RED-HAIRED
Ron's face print on the reverse of Reg's head smiles awkwardly. It's from the moment when the potion wears off and the real Reg arrives as Mary kisses who she thinks is her husband.

SMOOTH RUNNING
The Ministry of Magic is kept in order by the Magical Maintenance Department, from mopping the floors to deciding what weather the enchanted windows will show.

ALBERT RUNCORN
MINISTRY HUNTER OF MUGGLE-BORNS

Hard expression shows his aggressive attitude to Muggle-born witches and wizards

Ministry pin on lapel

TWO-FACED
Harry's cover is blown when the Polyjuice Potion wears off. Runcorn's minifigure head turns to reveal Harry's alarmed face, and his minifigure comes with Harry's hair piece.

IN PLAIN SIGHT
Harry poses as the intimidating Runcorn to get into the Ministry building. It's easy to walk around the Ministry unchallenged if you're someone people are afraid of.

Long black leather jacket over business suit

BY HARRY'S SEVENTH YEAR, the Ministry has fallen to Voldemort. Some employees stay on to try and improve matters, but many are under threat themselves. Others, like Albert Runcorn are actively working to arrest and imprison Muggle-borns.

MAGICAL FILE

YEAR: 2022
SET: 76403: The Ministry of Magic
ACCESSORIES: Wand

CORBAN YAXLEY
DEATH EATER IN THE MINISTRY

Long blonde hair is scraped back into a low ponytail and is in this color for the first time

MAGICAL FILE

YEAR: 2022

SET: 76403: The Ministry of Magic

ACCESSORIES: Wand

Fancy expensive robes show Yaxley's taste for luxury and power

A DEATH EATER IN Voldemort's inner circle, Corban Yaxley is controlling the Minister of Magic with the Imperious Curse. As Head of the Department of Magical Law Enforcement, he aims to rid the magical world of all those who aren't pure-bloods.

Golden pocket watch—Yaxley times Reg by giving him an hour to fix the rain in his office

MOST WANTED

The Ministry is printing anti-Muggle propaganda along with stacks of fliers that declare Harry to be "Undesirable No. 1" and offer a 10,000-Galleon reward for him.

DECOY DETONATOR

In this Ministry set, three tiny LEGO® elements make up the Decoy Detonators that Harry uses to create a diversion. They scuttle away then produce alarming bangs and smoke.

179

PIUS THICKNESSE
PUPPET MINISTER OF MAGIC

PIUS THICKNESSE WAS
an ordinary but influential Ministry employee until the Death Eater Corban Yaxley put him under his control with the Imperious Curse. Now he is Minister for Magic, but he's really a puppet, controlled by Lord Voldemort.

Troubled brow because Thicknesse's mind is being controlled

Ministry pin on tie

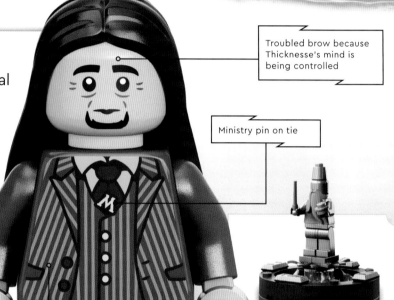

Pin-stripe three-piece suit marks him out as most senior wizard in the Ministry

HATE FIGURE
A new statue, "Magic is Might," replaces the Fountain of Magical Brethren—a physical demonstration of the regime's pure-blood superiority and lack of tolerance to others.

MAGICAL FILE

YEAR: 2022
SET: 76403: The Ministry of Magic
ACCESSORIES: Brown briefcase with Time-Turner, wand

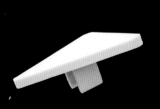

WIZARD MEMOS
Employees in the Ministry communicate with each other with flying interdepartmental memos. They used to use owls, but there was too much mess—droppings all over the desks!

MARY CATTERMOLE
WITCH ON TRIAL

Hair piece is a black version of Supergirl's blonde hair and Poison Ivy's red hair from the LEGO DC Super Heroes theme

Alternative face looks terrified because of her trial hearing

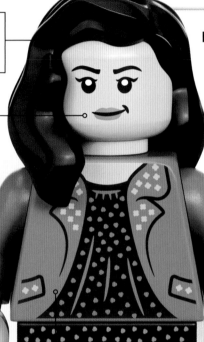

MAGICAL FILE

YEAR: 2022

SET: 76403: The Ministry of Magic

ACCESSORIES: None

LIKE MANY WITCHES and wizards, Mary Cattermole was Muggle-born. Now that Dark forces have taken over the Ministry, those with Muggle blood are not considered acceptable any more. Because of this, Mary is on trial and faces Azkaban.

Blazer and black dress are respectable for court

SHOW TRIAL
Head of the Muggle-Born Registration Commission, Dolores Umbridge presides over Mary's case. Her cat Patronus keeps her safe from the Dementors who patrol the courtroom.

DID YOU KNOW?
Mary is married to Ministry worker Reg Cattermole. Their children are Maisie, Ellie, and Alfred. When her trial is disrupted by Harry, Ron, and Hermione, she escapes but it's not safe to go home.

GRIPHOOK
GOBLIN FROM GRINGOTTS WIZARDING BANK

Sword of Gryffindor ultimately belongs to goblins in Griphook's view because it was goblin-made

Pointed ears, molded to hair piece, clip onto a regular minifigure head

Sharp, spiked teeth

SAFE KEEPING
Griphook first met Harry on the boy's first visit to Diagon Alley, just before his first year. Hagrid brought Harry to Gringotts for his gold, and the goblin accompanied him in the cart to his vault.

BANK TELLER
In the 2021 Harry Potter Advent Calendar (76390), Griphook wears a red version of the Gringotts uniform he was in when he first met Harry.

GOBLINS HAVE a hard time because their culture and code of honor clash with those of wizards and witches. No wonder Griphook is cranky. He helps Harry break into Gringotts, but the consequences of making a deal with a goblin are always unpredictable.

MAGICAL FILE

YEAR: 2020

SET: 71028: LEGO Harry Potter Minifigures Series 2

ACCESSORIES: Sword of Gryffindor, key

THE GRAY LADY
GHOST OF RAVENCLAW TOWER

First gray version of Luna Lovegood's blonde hair piece

Young, beautiful face is wracked with regret

MAGICAL FILE

YEAR: 2023

SET: 76413: Hogwarts™ Room of Requirement

ACCESSORIES: Sword of Gryffindor

Witch's robes from a thousand years ago

THE THIRD GHOSTLY minifigure in the Harry Potter theme, the Gray Lady is the ghost of Ravenclaw. Born Helena, she suffered a tragic life and death marred by jealousy and rage. Ravenclaw house was named after her mother, Rowena Ravenclaw.

GRAY AREA
No person alive has seen the Lost Diadem of Ravenclaw, but a ghost can help Harry destroy it: he tracks down shy Helena to discover its history and clues to its current location.

DID YOU KNOW?
Helena jealously stole Ravenclaw's enchanted diadem from her mother. For centuries it was known only as the Lost Diadem of Ravenclaw, but Tom Riddle coaxed its hiding place from Helena and turned it into a Horcrux.

VOLDEMORT

HE WHO MUST NOT BE NAMED

Snakelike facial features

MAGICAL FILE

YEAR: 2018

SET: 71022 LEGO Harry Potter Minifigures Series 1

ACCESSORIES: Nagini, wand

Hand can clasp Nagini's tail

NOW IN SNAKE-GREEN robes, Voldemort is stronger than ever. He has torn his soul into pieces and hidden them in seven objects called Horcruxes. Harry destroys as many as he can, then they meet face to face. A prophecy says only one can survive...

Green robes first worn when battling Dumbledore in the Ministry of Magic at the end of Harry's fifth year

ARMY RECRUITS

In his bid to take over the magical world, Voldemort has been enlisting many dangerous creatures for his cause, including the Dementors who previously guarded Azkaban prison.

NAGINI

Voldemort keeps his giant snake close by. More than a pet, Nagini is a Horcrux, so she has part of the Dark Lord's soul. He can talk with her telepathically and even possess her body.

NEVILLE LONGBOTTOM

HORCRUX SLAYER

Sword of Gryffindor imbued with Basilisk venom can destroy Horcruxes

Buck teeth in an expression of brave determination

FIRE STORM

Fiendfyre is no ordinary fire. Its enchanted flames mutate into fiery beasts like snakes and dragons. It's deadly and wild, but it does destroy the Diadem Horcrux.

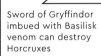

DID YOU KNOW?

The Battle of Hogwarts takes place when Voldemort and his Death Eaters storm their way into the school. The conflict is not without casualties, but it marks the end of the Second Wizarding War.

Fair Isle knitted cardigan is unusual battle attire

MAGICAL FILE

YEAR: 2022
SET: 76404: LEGO Harry Potter™ Advent Calendar
ACCESSORIES: Sword of Gryffindor

THE TIME HAS COME for Dumbledore's Army to fight. As the Battle of Hogwarts rages, bruised and battered Neville has a special task: to destroy Nagini—Voldemort's snake and the last Horcrux. Then the Dark Lord will finally become vulnerable.

THE NEXT GENERATION

HARRY'S OWN FAMILY

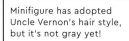
Minifigure has adopted Uncle Vernon's hair style, but it's not gray yet!

Stubble for the first time on a Harry minifigure

Denim jeans make Harry's shirt and blazer more casual

NINETEEN YEARS AFTER defeating Voldemort once and for all, Harry is back at King's Cross on the first of September for the departure of the Hogwarts Express. But this time he isn't a passenger—he's dropping off his own children.

HARRY POTTER

Now an Auror—a Dark wizard hunter—Harry is married to Ginny Weasley. Ron and Hermione also work for the Ministry, and Hermione rises to the top job, as Minister for Magic.

Straight hair gotten wavier with age

More freckles than when she was younger

Leather jacket

MAGICAL FILE

YEAR: 2022

SET: 76405: Hogwarts Express—Collector's Edition

ACCESSORIES: N/A

GINNY POTTER

After Hogwarts, Ginny went into journalism and now she travels all around the world in her capacity as special Quidditch correspondent for the *Daily Prophet*.

Hair piece is even more unkempt than Harry's used to be

Casual clothes will be changed for Gryffindor robes once James is onboard

Hair piece from his Uncle Ron but in the same color as Harry's hair

Casual clothes soon to be replaced with house robes after the Sorting Ceremony

JAMES SIRIUS POTTER

Named after Harry's father and godfather, James is confidently looking forward to going back to school. He's eager to get on the train and leave his brother and sister behind.

As the oldest child, James is the only one in the family with a three-quarter-size leg piece

ALBUS SEVERUS POTTER

This is Albus's first trip to Hogwarts and he's nervous about what's in store. Two years younger than his big brother, Albus was named after two great headmasters of Hogwarts.

Hair pulled back in a clip, just like Ginny's used to be

Face print shared with her mom's first-year minifigure

LILY LUNA POTTER

Lily, named after her grandmother, is the youngest. Like her mother before her, she has to watch all her brothers head off to school before it's her turn. She still has another two years to wait.

Short leg piece because Lily is the youngest minifigure in the LEGO Harry Potter theme to date

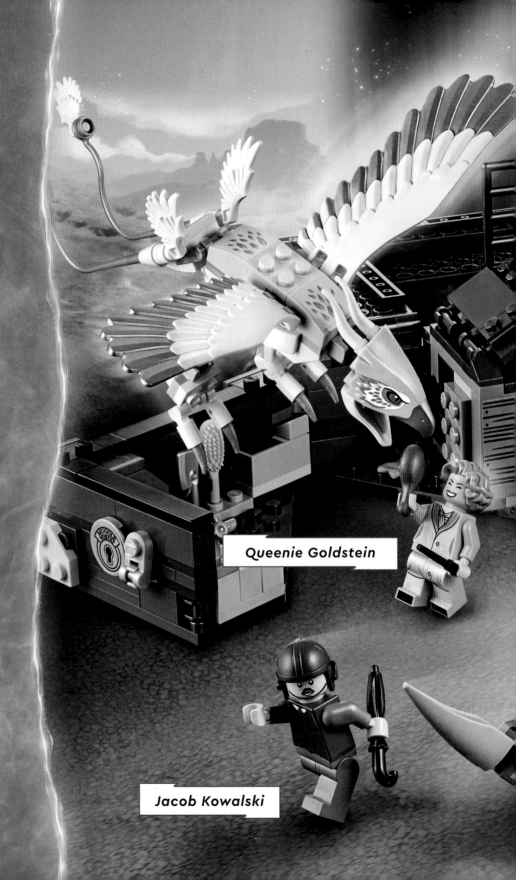

Queenie Goldstein

Jacob Kowalski

I NEED TO FIND EVERYONE WHO'S ESCAPED, BEFORE THEY GET HURT.

Newt Scamander

Tina Goldstein

EVERY HOGWARTS STUDENT KNOWS the textbook *Fantastic Beasts and Where to Find Them*, but few know much about its author. 100 years ago, Newt Scamander was a passionate Magizoologist intent on educating people about all the wonderful creatures in the magical world.

NEWT SCAMANDER

MAGIZOOLOGIST

IN THE 1920S, Newt Scamander is a Magizoologist—he studies, rescues, and protects magical creatures and tries to educate his fellow wizards about them. He's even writing a book called *Fantastic Beasts and Where to Find Them*.

Nifflers are little furry animals who can't resist hording anything shiny

MAGICAL FILE

YEAR: 2018

SET: 71022: LEGO Harry Potter Minifigures Series 1

ACCESSORIES: Case, Niffler

HOME SWEET HOME
Newt travels to New York with his case, which has more to it than meets the eye. Within is his workshop as well as varied habitats for many species of creatures to live and roam.

Case uses the LEGO book cover piece for lid

CARER OF MAGICAL CREATURES
Here Newt's minifigure is in his shirt sleeves, ready to get to work with the animals. He has his work cut out feeding, reassuring, grooming, and keeping them healthy and safe.

TINA GOLDSTEIN

AUROR FOR MACUSA

1920s-style cloche hat is attached to hair piece

Alternative face print looks annoyed

PORPENTINA "TINA" GOLDSTEIN

works with MACUSA —the Magical Congress of the United States of America. On the streets of New York, she fights Dark magic and enforces the Statute of Secrecy to keep Muggles unaware of her community.

CITY SAFARI

Without her overcoat or hat, Tina helps find the animals on the loose from Newt's Case of Magical Creatures (75952). They definitely contravene the Statute of Secrecy!

Hotdog is being eaten when Tina first bumps into Newt Scamander

MAGICAL FILE

YEAR: 2018

SET: 71022: LEGO Harry Potter Minifigures Series 1

ACCESSORIES: Hotdog, wand

OCCAMY

The vibrant Occamy changes size to fill the space available, be it a huge department store or a tiny container. When one escapes Newt's case, Tina tempts it into a teapot to shrink and capture it.

QUEENIE GOLDSTEIN
AMERICAN LEGILIMENS

QUEENIE WORKS FOR MACUSA like her sister, Tina, but in the less dangerous Wand Permit Office. As a Legilimens, she can read other people's minds. This makes her kind and sensitive to people's feelings, but she can also use it to her advantage.

MAGICAL FILE

YEAR: 2018
SET: 71022: LEGO Harry Potter Minifigures Series 1
ACCESSORIES: Wand, strudel

Apple-and-raisin strudel assembled and baked by wand

Uneven hemlines are popular during the 1920s

Dual molded legs with printed black high-heels that sweep up on the side of the feet

EXPLOSIVE CREATURE
Rhino-like Erumpents like open plains, trees, and water, so when loose in New York, Newt's Erumpent heads to Central Park. When it's returned to Newt's case, Queenie feeds it.

TICKLED PINK
Queenie's minifigure, overprinted with shades of pink, helps Newt track down his animals. She wears a 1920s-style pink coat with a wide velvet collar.

JACOB KOWALSKI

A NO-MAJ NEW YORKER

Hair piece is a darker brown version of Cedric Diggory's

Tidy suit in attempt to impress bank manager and get a loan for his bakery

ERUMPENT TARGET

Newt's escaped Erumpent takes a liking to Jacob and chases him across Central Park—thankfully Jacob has a padded jacket and a helmet with a chin strap.

MAGICAL FILE

YEAR: 2018

SET: 71022: LEGO Harry Potter Minifigures Series 1

ACCESSORIES: Suitcase with two pastries

JACOB KOWALSKI is a No-Maj—the American term for a Muggle—who dreams of opening a bakery. He's staggered to discover the magical world when he runs into Newt Scamander and becomes embroiled in magical happenings.

Case exterior looks so similar to Newt's that they get muddled up

THUNDERBIRD RIDE

The real reason Newt has come to America is to return Frank, a Thunderbird. Newt found him chained up in Egypt and is bringing him back to the wilds of Arizona where he belongs.

PERCIVAL GRAVES
PAWN OF GRINDELWALD

Hair piece printed gray around the bottom

Alternative face is Grindelwald's with white eyebrows and mustache

DID YOU KNOW?
Graves has such a senior position at MACUSA that when he orders the execution of Tina Goldstein and Newt Scamander, nobody questions him. Fortunately, the pair escape and eventually uncover his true identity.

EVEN THOUGH PERCIVAL GRAVES is MACUSA's Director of Magical Security, he can't keep himself or America safe. The Dark wizard Gellert Grindelwald uses Human Transfiguration to impersonate Graves and infiltrate the American Ministry for Magic.

Outfit is a cross between formal office wear and wizarding robes, with a 1920s twist

BODY OF EVIDENCE
In the first series of Harry Potter Minifigures, Graves' minifigure comes with clues—a white hair piece and, if you turn his head around, a face print of Gellert Grindelwald!

MAGICAL FILE

YEAR: 2018
SET: 71022: LEGO Harry Potter Minifigures Series 1
ACCESSORIES: Wand

GELLERT GRINDELWALD
DARK WIZARD

White version of Draco's swept-back hair piece

Face doesn't have mustache, unlike Grindelwald's first minifigure

MAGICAL FILE

YEAR: 2018
SET: 75951: Grindelwald's Escape
ACCESSORIES: Wand, shooting spell

High-waisted trousers with printed decoration

A GENERATION BEFORE

Voldemort, there was another name feared above all others: Gellert Grindelwald. In the 1920s, he wants to break the Statute of Secrecy, provoke war, and create a regime where wizards and witches rule over Muggles.

DID YOU KNOW?

Grindelwald went to school at the Durmstrang Institute. When he was younger—before the full extent of his intentions were revealed—he was a very close friend of Albus Dumbledore.

FREE WIZARD

While in MACUSA custody, Grindelwald is due to be transported by high-security Incarceration Carriage from prison to face trial in Europe. Instead, he engineers his escape.

Senior Editor Laura Palosuo
Senior Art Editor David McDonald
Senior US Editor Megan Douglass
Production Editor Siu Yin Chan
Senior Production Controller Lloyd Robertson
Managing Editor Paula Regan
Managing Art Editor Jo Connor
Publishing Director Mark Searle

Packaged for DK by Dynamo Limited
Publishing Manager Claire Lister
Design Project Manager Andrew Fishleigh

Dorling Kindersley would like to thank
Ashley Blais, Randi K. Sørensen, Heidi K. Jensen,
Paul Hansford, and Martin Leighton Lindhardt
at the LEGO Group;
Kurtis Estes, Victoria Selover, and Katie Campbell
at Warner Bros. Consumer Products and
Luke Barnard from The Blair Partnership.

First American Edition, 2023
Published in the United States by DK Publishing
1745 Broadway, 20th Floor, New York, NY 10019

Page design copyright © 2023 Dorling Kindersley Limited
A Penguin Random House Company

LEGO, the LEGO logo, the Minifigure,
and the Brick and Knob configurations
are trademarks of the LEGO Group.
© 2023 the LEGO Group.

Manufactured by Dorling Kindersley,
One Embassy Gardens,
8 Viaduct Gardens, London SW11 7BW,
under license from the LEGO Group.

This book was made with Forest
Stewardship Council™ certified
paper—one small step in DK's
commitment to a sustainable future.
For more information go to
www.dk.com/our-green-pledge

23 24 25 26 27 10 9 8 7 6 5 4 3 2 1
001–333495–July/2023

A catalog record for this book
is available from the Library of Congress.
Hardcover ISBN: 978-0-7440-8174-9
Library edition ISBN: 978-0-7440-8175-6

Printed and bound in China

For the curious
www.dk.com
www.LEGO.com